Excel

Get the Results You Want!

Years 5–6
Selective Schools
and
Scholarship Tests

Sharon Dalgleish,
Tanya Dalgleish, Donna
Gibbs, Allyn Jones &
Hamish McLean

PASCAL
PRESS

© 2022 Sharon Dalgleish, Tanya Dalgleish, Donna Gibbs, Allyn Jones, Hamish McLean and Pascal Press

Completely new edition incorporating late 2020 Selective School test changes

Reprinted 2023, 2024

ISBN 978 1 74125 630 7

Pascal Press Pty Ltd
PO Box 250
Glebe NSW 2037
(02) 9198 1748
www.pascalpress.com.au

Publisher: Vivienne Joannou
Project editor: Mark Dixon
Edited by Mark Dixon and Rosemary Peers
Mathematical Reasoning section co-written by James Athanasou
Writing section written by Alan Horsfield
Answers checked by Dale Little and Peter Little
Cover by DiZign Pty Ltd
Typeset by Grizzly Graphics (Leanne Richters)
Printed by Vivar Printing/Green Giant Press

Contents

Sample tests

Answers

ADVICE ON PREPARING FOR THE TESTS

The following points summarise some general advice on preparing for the tests:

- Familiarity with a test helps to overcome some nerves.
- There is no best way to prepare for these types of tests. It certainly helps to be a capable reader and to have strong general knowledge. It is also a good sign if you are able to analyse and solve different types of problems easily.
- This book contains 16 test papers—four sample tests for each subject—to help you prepare for the tests.

BACKGROUND TO SELECTIVE TESTING

Tests for entry into selective government schools were introduced in order to provide an opportunity for pupils with scholastic aptitude. Over 15 000 applications are made for the just over 4000 selective places available and entry is quite competitive. It is not unusual for some primary schools not to be able to place even one of their pupils into a selective school.

The tests were updated in 2020 with a greater emphasis on literacy, critical-thinking skills, mathematical reasoning and problem solving. The General Ability test has been replaced by a Thinking Skills test. The new Selective High School Placement Test adjusts and balances the weighting given to the Reading, Thinking Skills, Mathematical Reasoning and Writing components. These changes were in response to the findings of the 2018 Review of Selective Education Access report, commissioned by the NSW Department of Education.

ABOUT THE SELECTIVE SCHOOL TEST

The NSW Selective High School Placement Test consists of four sections:

- **Reading** (30 questions in 40 minutes)
- **Thinking Skills** (40 questions in 40 minutes)
- **Mathematical Reasoning** (35 questions in 40 minutes)
- **Writing** (one question in 30 minutes).

The tests, except Writing, are in multiple-choice form, with each question being of equal value. Marks are awarded for each correct answer and applicants are advised to guess the answer if they are uncertain.

Although there are similarities in the content of the NSW Selective High School Placement Test and the ACER Scholarship Tests, since the Selective Schools Test format changed in 2020 there are now more differences.

HOW THE RESULTS ARE USED BY PUBLIC SCHOOLS

Entry to selective high schools is based on academic merit. In 2022 changes were made to the allocation of places. Under the Equity Placement Model, up to 20% of places are held for members of the following disadvantaged and under-represented groups:

- students from low socio-educational advantage backgrounds
- First Nations students
- rural and remote students
- students with disability.

It is important to remember that the places allocated under the Equity Placement Model will not necessarily be filled. In 2023, the first year of this new system, less than 10% of these places were offered. This means that more than 90% of the places were offered to general applicants. The new system has helped close the educational gap in participation from disadvantaged groups without having a significant impact on other applicants.

Students no longer receive a test score or placement rank. The new performance report will instead place students in one of the following categories:

- top 10% of candidates
- next 15% of candidates
- next 25% of candidates
- lowest 50% of candidates.

This change addresses privacy and wellbeing concerns including unhealthy competition between students. The sole purpose of the test is to identify students who would benefit from the chance to study at a selective school and, since it doesn't test knowledge of the curriculum, there is no diagnostic merit in the test—unlike the NAPLAN test, which can help identify areas where children can improve.

Minimum entry scores for selective schools are no longer published because these change from year to year and depend on the number of applicants, their relative performance and the number of families who decline an offer. Students placed on the reserve list no longer receive a numerical rank; instead an indication of how long it will take to receive an offer, based on previous years, is provided.

A selection committee for each selective high school decides which students are to be offered places. These committees also decide how many students are to be placed on the reserve list. Should a student with a confirmed offer turn down a place at a selective school, the place will be offered to the first student on the reserve list.

There is an appeals panel for illness or other mitigating circumstances. All applicants are advised of the outcome. The NSW Government provides detailed information on the application and selection process for parents on the Selective High School Placement Test. This is available from: https://education.nsw.gov.au/parents-and-carers/learning/tests-and-exams/selective-school-test. Sample test papers are also available on this website.

ABOUT THE SCHOLARSHIP TESTS

The ACER Scholarship Tests, which are usually held around May, are coordinated by the Australian Council for Educational Research (ACER). This testing is for entry to around 200 independent schools. About 15 000 students throughout Australia sit these tests. The tests cover three levels:

- Level 1: the last year of primary school (Year 6)
- Level 2: the second year of high school (Year 8)
- Level 3: Year 10 in high school.

Each private school awards its own scholarships. You can put your name down for more than one school but you will need a special registration form. There is also a separate fee for each school and you lodge your registration directly with the school and not with ACER.

You may be limited in the number of schools to which you can apply. This might happen if a school insists you have to sit for the test at their testing centre. Candidates usually sit the exam at the school which is their first choice. There are exceptions for country and interstate candidates.

The ACER Scholarship Tests comprise:
- Test 1: Written Expression (25 minutes)

- Test 2: Humanities—Comprehension and Interpretation (40 minutes)
- Test 3: Mathematics (40 minutes)
- Test 4: Written Expression (25 minutes).

HOW THE RESULTS ARE USED BY PRIVATE SCHOOLS

The results are used by private schools to select students who have applied for a scholarship. Typically the highest scorers are considered first, together with any additional background information that might have been provided. It is important therefore to provide as much detail as possible in the application form to assist the selection committee in deciding between pupils who may have similar scores.

ADVICE TO PARENTS/ GUARDIANS

Every child has their own talents which need to be discovered and nurtured. Some children are high achievers or have special talents which are not reflected in the results of these tests.

This is because these tests focus on predicting the overall educational achievement of high scorers but may not be accurate in predicting how well a particular pupil might perform. In fact some pupils with high scores in these tests may not ultimately do well in high school while some who were not selected will go on to attain excellent academic results.

Children need to be interested in undertaking these tests. This will be a significant and memorable event for them and they need support as the tests are very competitive.

It is advisable that children should not undertake the NSW Selective High School Placement Test unless some of the following criteria are satisfied:

- they are among the top of their class at school
- they attend an Opportunity Class
- they are very good at English and Mathematics
- they read widely
- it is their decision to apply for a selective school
- the preparation for the test is not stressful for them.

This book is designed to give an opportunity for your child to become familiar with the format and style of the test questions.

Suggested procedure:

- Complete the first test.
- Keep a record of your times and accuracy.
- Repeat each test until you get **all** the questions correct.
- Keep on repeating each test until you are familiar with it.
- Keep on repeating each test until the time it takes you to finish the test is as fast as possible.
- Now repeat this with the next test.
- Then, when you are confident, you can complete the next test.

Keep in mind that some question types may require more practice than others. You might need more time initially to complete these sorts of questions. Some of the more challenging Thinking Skills problem-solving questions, for example, could take you up to 15 minutes to complete to begin with, as you may use diagrams or tables to help you solve them. Remember that the more questions you do of this same type, the faster you will become—until you know exactly how to solve them.

In the next section there are four sample tests each for Reading, Thinking Skills, Mathematical Reasoning and Writing. There are answers as well as brief explanations of the correct answers in order to help you.

ADVICE TO STUDENTS

The tests are difficult and you may not finish them in the time available. Don't worry about this because many students will also find the questions very hard. You can't learn the answers to the questions in these tests like you can with some school tests because they force you to deal with new situations.

We wish you all the best in the tests and hope these notes will be of some help in making you familiar with the different types of questions in the test and helping you increase your speed and accuracy. Don't worry if you don't get a place because there are thousands and thousands of applicants. Just give it your best shot.

Here is a summary of the advice that the Education Department and ACER give to people taking the tests:

- There is nothing special that you have to learn in order to do these tests.
- These are tests to see whether you can think clearly with words and numbers.
- Listen carefully to the instructions.
- If you are not sure what to do then ask.
- Make sure you know where to mark the answers for each test.
- Do not open the test booklet until you are told.
- Read each question carefully before giving your answer.
- There is no penalty for guessing—so guess if you are not sure.

- Don't rush—work steadily and as carefully as you can.
- If a question is too hard, don't worry—come back to it later if you have time.
- It is easy to get your answers out of order, so always check the number of the question you are answering.
- Every now and then make sure the answer is in the correctly numbered circle.
- Feel free to write on the question booklet for any rough working.
- Don't do any rough work on the answer sheet.
- If you want to change an answer, rub it out and fill in the appropriate circle for your new answer.
- Keep track of the time—you will not be told when time is running out.
- Don't fold the answer sheet—it has to be put through a machine to mark it.

For the NSW Selective High School Placement Test you will need:

- a good pencil rubber (one that doesn't smudge)
- a HB or B pencil (don't use pens or biros)
- a spare pencil.

For the ACER Scholarship Tests you will need:

- a good pencil rubber (one that doesn't smudge)
- a HB or B pencil (for the answer sheet)
- a spare pencil
- two blue or black pens for the Writing Test.

Reading answer sheet

Mark your answers here.

To answer each question, fill in the appropriate circle for your chosen answer.

Use a pencil. If you make a mistake or change your mind, erase and try again.

You can make extra copies of this answer sheet to mark your answers to all the Sample Reading tests in this book.

	A B C D		A B C D		A B C D
1	○○○○	11	○○○○	21	○○○○
2	A B C D ○○○○	12	A B C D ○○○○	22	A B C D ○○○○
3	A B C D ○○○○	13	A B C D ○○○○	23	A B C D ○○○○
4	A B C D ○○○○	14	A B C D ○○○○	24	A B C D ○○○○
5	A B C D ○○○○	15	A B C D E F G ○○○○○○○	25	A B C D ○○○○
6	A B C D ○○○○	16	A B C D E F G ○○○○○○○	26	A B C D ○○○○
7	A B C D ○○○○	17	A B C D E F G ○○○○○○○	27	A B C D ○○○○
8	A B C D ○○○○	18	A B C D E F G ○○○○○○○	28	A B C D ○○○○
9	A B C D ○○○○	19	A B C D E F G ○○○○○○○	29	A B C D ○○○○
10	A B C D ○○○○	20	A B C D E F G ○○○○○○○	30	A B C D ○○○○

Thinking Skills answer sheet

Mark your answers here.

To answer each question, fill in the appropriate circle for your chosen answer.

Use a pencil. If you make a mistake or change your mind, erase and try again.

You can make extra copies of this answer sheet to mark your answers to all the Sample Thinking Skills tests in this book.

	A B C D		A B C D		A B C D		A B C D
1	○○○○	11	○○○○	21	○○○○	31	○○○○
2	○○○○	12	○○○○	22	○○○○	32	○○○○
3	○○○○	13	○○○○	23	○○○○	33	○○○○
4	○○○○	14	○○○○	24	○○○○	34	○○○○
5	○○○○	15	○○○○	25	○○○○	35	○○○○
6	○○○○	16	○○○○	26	○○○○	36	○○○○
7	○○○○	17	○○○○	27	○○○○	37	○○○○
8	○○○○	18	○○○○	28	○○○○	38	○○○○
9	○○○○	19	○○○○	29	○○○○	39	○○○○
10	○○○○	20	○○○○	30		40	○○○○

Mathematical Reasoning answer sheet

Mark your answers here.

To answer each question, fill in the appropriate circle for your chosen answer.

Use a pencil. If you make a mistake or change your mind, erase and try again.

You can make extra copies of this answer sheet to mark your answers to all the Sample Mathematical Reasoning tests in this book.

	A B C D E		A B C D E		A B C D E		A B C D E		A B C D E
1	○○○○○	8	○○○○○	15	○○○○○	22	○○○○○	29	○○○○○
2	○○○○○	9	○○○○○	16	○○○○○	23	○○○○○	30	○○○○○
3	○○○○○	10	○○○○○	17	○○○○○	24	○○○○○	31	○○○○○
4	○○○○○	11	○○○○○	18	○○○○○	25	○○○○○	32	○○○○○
5	○○○○○	12	○○○○○	19	○○○○○	26	○○○○○	33	○○○○○
6	○○○○○	13	○○○○○	20	○○○○○	27	○○○○○	34	○○○○○
7	○○○○○	14	○○○○○	21	○○○○○	28	○○○○○	35	○○○○○

SAMPLE TEST 1

Read the texts below then answer the questions.

TEXT 1

The Adventures of Theseus

The Athenians were compelled to surrender to Minos and they had to agree to the most humiliating terms. They promised to send seven youths and seven maidens every year to Crete.

Now Minos had a park laid out by the most cunning man of his times. There were walks and paths so many and so winding that no-one who got into it could get out again but had to wander on and on, getting more and more confused. This park was called the Labyrinth and in the centre of it was a cave in which just at that time King Minos kept a dangerous monster which had the body and limbs of a man but the head of a bull.

The creature was called the Minotaur and it was fierce and cruel. There was only one way to prevent him from roaming the fields and endangering the lives of the people. He had to be kept in a good humour and this could be done only by feeding him now and then on human flesh. So Minos bethought him of using the Athenian captives for that purpose.

The ship reached Crete and Minos ordered the weeping youths and maidens to be thrown into the den of the Minotaur and Theseus with them. (Theseus chose to go with the captives as he wanted to defend his family honour.) By a lucky chance Ariadne, the daughter of the king, saw Theseus and was moved with pity and a wish to save him. She slyly gave him a ball of yarn and told him to fasten one end of it to the inside entrance to the Labyrinth and then wind it off as he walked along that he might find his way back again.

Theseus took the ball and went with his companions into the Labyrinth. He fastened one end of the thread firmly to the inside of the entrance and, as he walked along, the thread caught and held onto the bushes. They could hear the bellowing of the Minotaur as they approached the cave and the companions of Theseus hid themselves in the bushes, trembling with fright. But Theseus approached fearlessly and, rushing upon the Minotaur, thrust his sword through him and the monster fell dead.

The youths and maidens came out from their hiding places and, surrounding Theseus, kissed his hands and called him their preserver. Theseus, guided by the thread which Ariadne had given him, led his companions safely to the entrance of the Labyrinth. And when they were free from its entanglements, Theseus gratefully raised up his hands to heaven and offered a prayer of thanks to the gods for their escape.

From 'The Adventures of Theseus' by Mary E Burtrand and ZA Ragozin

TEXT 2

The Heroes

Then Athené smiled and said—

'They [the three Gray Sisters] will tell you the way to the Gorgon that you may slay her, my enemy, the mother of monstrous beasts. Once she was a maiden as beautiful as morn, till in her pride she sinned a sin at which the sun hid his face; and from that day her hair was turned to vipers, and her hands to eagle's claws; and her heart was filled with shame and rage, and her lips with bitter venom; and her eyes became so terrible that whosoever looks on them is turned to stone …

'You shall take this polished shield,' said Athené, 'and when you come near her look not at her herself, but at her image in the brass; so you may strike her safely. And when you have struck off her head, wrap it, with your face turned away, in the folds of the goatskin on which the shield hangs, the hide of Amaltheié, the nurse of the Ægis-holder. So you will bring it safely back to me and win to yourself renown, and a place among the heroes who feast with the Immortals upon the peak where no winds blow.'

[Time passes and after enormous struggles amidst great dangers, Perseus slays the Gorgon.]

Then Perseus went out, and up to the hall of Polydectes; and underneath the goatskin he bore the Gorgon's head.

'Those whom the Gods help fulfil their promises; and those who despise them, reap as they have sown. Behold the Gorgon's head!'

Then Perseus drew back the goatskin and held aloft the Gorgon's head.

Pale grew Polydectes and his guests as they looked upon that dreadful face. They tried to rise up from their seats: but from their seats they never rose, but stiffened, each man where he sat, into a ring of cold gray stones.

From *The Heroes* by Charles Kingsley

SAMPLE TEST 1

For questions **1–8**, choose the option (**A**, **B**, **C** or **D**) which you think best answers the question.

1 In which text does catching sight of someone by chance play an important part?
 A Text 1
 B Text 2
 C Both
 D Neither

2 Both texts are about
 A men who kill other men.
 B men who act heroically.
 C women who act heroically.
 D women who feel pity.

3 Which main quality, other than bravery, makes Theseus heroic?
 A common sense
 B obedience
 C intelligence
 D unselfishness

4 What do Ariadne and Athene have in common?
 A They are both princesses.
 B They are both close to the Immortals.
 C They are both beautiful and intelligent.
 D They both give good advice.

5 In which text is there a creature that is part human and part animal?
 A Text 1
 B Text 2
 C Both
 D Neither

6 What made Minos confident?
 A his Labyrinth
 B the obedience of the Athenians
 C his minotaur
 D the loyalty of his daughter

7 Perseus's words, 'Behold the Gorgon's head!', create a moment of
 A relief.
 B light relief.
 C high tension.
 D anticlimax.

8 How do Polydectes and his guests feel when they look at the Gorgon's head?
 A scared
 B petrified
 C frightened
 D worried

SAMPLE TEST 1

Read the poem below by Donna Gibbs then answer the questions.

Friendship?

She was there again.
We looked at each other across the road.
Me through our green wire gate.
She from her front steps.
How did we cross that space?
I can't remember.
She didn't have a mother
so she used mine.
She'd bring her brush and rubber bands
    over in the morning.
My mum would do our hair
before we walked to school together.
Sometimes when she came over in the
    holidays
I'd want to hide
because I wanted to be alone
talking to my imaginary friends.
Other times when we went to the beach
we'd have the best of times.
My dad would whirl us around.
First one. Then the other.
Our feet slicing through the sea.
And we'd sing White Christmas in the car
    coming home.
She always licked her ice cream more
    slowly than I did.
Then she'd make the most of what she
    had left
when I had none.

© Donna Gibbs; reproduced with permission

For questions **9–14**, choose the option (**A**, **B**, **C** or **D**) which you think best answers the question.

9 Who is 'She' in the first line of the poem?
A the narrator
B the girl's mother
C the girl from across the road
D the narrator's mother

10 When was the girls' relationship at its best?
A at its beginning
B when getting their hair done together
C on beach trips
D when eating ice cream

11 What does the the choice of the word 'used' suggest the narrator is feeling about the girl's behaviour?
A uncomfortable
B angry
C pleased
D sad

12 Which of these feelings is experienced by the narrator?
A hatred   B fury
C envy   D dislike

13 The 'friend' is presented in a _____ light.
A wholly sympathetic
B partly sympathetic
C very unsympathetic
D coldly unsympathetic

14 The question mark in the title is used to suggest the poet's
A uncertainty.
B anxiety.
C despair.
D confidence.

SAMPLE TEST 1

Read the text below then answer the questions.

Six sentences have been removed from the text. Choose from the sentences (**A–G**) the one which fits each gap (**15–20**). There is one extra sentence which you do not need to use.

The elephant

The elephant is the largest living land mammal. Unsurprisingly, it spends between 12 and 18 hours eating and drinking. **15** _____ It drinks an average-size bathtub full of water. An elephant does not have a very efficient digestive system and as a consequence produces large quantities of manure!

Elephants live in herds made up of family groups, usually of about eight to ten related females. **16** _____ When necessary, a matriarch will rely on the elephant's excellent memory to guide its herds to watering holes that have been visited in the past. The calves, usually one per elephant born after a 22-month gestation period, are cared for by the mother and other close females. When a male calf is somewhere between 12 and 15 years old, it leaves the group and usually lives a fairly solitary life.

The trunk of an elephant has multiple functions and is one of its most distinctive features. **17** _____ The trunk can sense vibrations coming towards it from a distance. It is strong enough to push down trees or lift extremely heavy weights. It is able to pick up both large and small things and to reach things at quite a distance. The trunk is used for greetings and caresses and plays an important part in the way elephants communicate with each other.

Elephants' tusks are their continuously growing front teeth. **18** _____ Over time, poaching of elephants to illegally gain ivory has led to the destruction of hundreds of thousands of elephants. The cruel methods used to kill these magnificent animals include shooting prey from helicopters or using machetes and spears spiked with cyanide.

In 1989, CITES (Convention on International Trade in Endangered Species of Wild Fauna and Flora) introduced a ban on the international trading of ivory. **19** _____ However, poaching and illegal trafficking of ivory appears to have gained ground again and is currently contributing to the endangerment of some species. **20** _____ However, three species—the African bush elephant, the African forest elephant and the Asian elephant—currently survive in the savannahs, forests, deserts and marshy areas of Africa and Asia.

A	The visible part of the tusk, the ivory, has always been in high demand.
B	These are led by the oldest female, the matriarch.
C	Elephants are afraid of things that move quickly around their feet such as mice.
D	Some species of elephant are now extinct.
E	This had some protective effects, as did the Chinese and American Presidents enacting ivory bans in their own countries.
F	It consumes large quantities of grasses, leaves, bamboo, bark, roots and other vegetation.
G	It uses it to breathe (its nostrils run the length of its trunk), feed, smell and bring water to its mouth and spray it over its body.

SAMPLE TEST 1

Read the four texts below on the theme of making history.

For questions **21–30**, choose the option (**A**, **B**, **C** or **D**) which you think best answers the question.

Which text …

expresses a strong sense of injustice?	21	_____
quotes words written in the 20th century?	22	_____
reveals a personal connection to history related to gender?	23	_____
includes many technical terms in its explanation?	24	_____
ends without fully revealing what happened to someone?	25	_____
includes a distressing answer to a question?	26	_____
explains how a better understanding was brought about?	27	_____
uses an adjective derived from the name of a Roman God famous for his strength?	28	_____
tries to persuade the reader to accept a personal viewpoint?	29	_____
refers to a world record of the time that helped shape political change?	30	_____

TEXT A

In the early 1890s an ambitious plan to gather signatures for a petition to get women the vote was undertaken in Victoria, Australia. It was a herculean task because the signatures had to be collected by hand and assembled into a document that could be delivered to parliament.

In 1891 The Women's Suffrage Petition, or the Monster Petition as it is known, was signed by 30 000 women. The petition was 260 metres long and 200 millimetres wide. The paper the signatures were written on was pasted onto calico then rolled onto a cardboard spindle. The petition was thought to be the largest in the world at that time.

Imagine my delight when, researching my family history, I discovered my great-grandmother and her sisters had signed this petition. I was able to look up the page and number of their signatures. My family had helped influence the movement towards women getting the vote!

TEXT B

Hi Grandad

This morning, 25 April, we held two minutes silence in our school assembly to honour the Anzacs who served at Gallipoli in World War I. Telling me about how your grandpa (my great-great-grandpa ☺) fought at Gallipoli really helped me understand what Anzac Day means. It all seemed long ago and far away to me before. But after you showed me your grandpa's diary from 1915, begun when he was only 18 and about to go to war, that changed.

His first entry stays in my mind:

'Sept 11 Will leave tonight for the Dardanelles.'

What must he have been feeling? We know the outcome but when he wrote this, everything that was to happen was ahead of him.

Mum said she'll text you with the time we'll be arriving next weekend.

Love, Samantha

TEXT C

Dear Diary

We've been studying the First Fleet at school. Today we learned about two of the youngest convicts on board.

Elizabeth Hayward was just 13 when the *Lady Penrhyn* set sail from Portsmouth to Australia with 101 female convicts. She'd stolen a gown, a bonnet and a bath cloak. Hey! I don't think the punishment fits the crime, do you?

John Hudson was only nine when he was sentenced to seven years transportation—and the judge wasn't certain he'd stolen anything! Here's the online transcript from his Old Bailey trial in 1793, dear Diary!

Court to Prisoner: *How old are you?* – John: *Going in nine.*
What business was you bred up in? – John: *None, sometimes a chimney sweeper.*
Have you any father or mother? – John: *Dead.*
How long ago? – John: *I do not know.*

He was kept prisoner on an old hulk for three years before joining the convicts on the *Friendship*. It made me feel very upset.

TEXT D

The gold first worked for in Australia, as in other places, was of course alluvial, by which is usually understood loose gold in nuggets, specks and dust, lying in drifts which were once the beds of long-extinct streams and rivers, or possibly the moraines of glaciers, as in New Zealand.

…

I hold, and hold strongly, that true alluvial gold is not always derived from the disintegration of lodes or reefs. For instance, the 'Welcome Nugget' certainly never came from a reef. No such mass of gold, or anything approaching it, has ever yet been taken from a quartz matrix. It was found at Bakery Hill, Ballarat, in 1858, weight 2195 ozs, and sold for £10 500. This was above its actual value.

The 'Welcome Stranger', a still-larger mass of gold, was found amongst the roots of a tree at Dunolly, Victoria, in 1869, by two starved-out fossickers named Deeson and Oates. The weight of this, the largest authenticated nugget ever found, was 2268½ ozs and it was sold for £10 000 but rendered useless as a specimen by the finders, who spent a night burning it to remove the adhering quartz.

From *Getting Gold* by JCF Johnson

Read the texts below then answer the questions.

TEXT 1

Jane Eyre

'And, ma'am,' he [Mr Brocklehurst] continued, 'the laundress tells me some of the girls have two clean tuckers in the week: it is too much; the rules limit them to one.'

… 'And there is another thing which surprised me; I find, in settling accounts with the housekeeper, that a lunch, consisting of bread and cheese, has twice been served out to the girls during the past fortnight. How is this? I looked over the regulations, and I find no such meal as lunch mentioned. Who introduced this innovation? and by what authority?'

'I must be responsible for the circumstance, sir,' replied Miss Temple: 'the breakfast was so ill prepared that the pupils could not possibly eat it; and I dared not allow them to remain fasting till dinner-time.'

'Madam, allow me an instant. You are aware that my plan in bringing up these girls is, not to accustom them to habits of luxury and indulgence, but to render them hardy, patient, self-denying …'

Meantime, Mr Brocklehurst, standing on the hearth with his hands behind his back, majestically surveyed the whole school. Suddenly his eye gave a blink, as if it had met something that either dazzled or shocked its pupil; turning, he said in more rapid accents than he had hitherto used—

'Miss Temple, Miss Temple, what—*what* is that girl with curled hair? Red hair, ma'am, curled—curled all over?' And extending his cane he pointed to the awful object, his hand shaking as he did so.

'It is Julia Severn,' replied Miss Temple, very quietly.

'Julia Severn, ma'am! And why has she, or any other, curled hair? Why, in defiance of every precept and principle of this house, does she conform to the world so openly—here in an evangelical, charitable establishment—as to wear her hair one mass of curls?'

'Julia's hair curls naturally,' returned Miss Temple, still more quietly …

I might have escaped notice, had not my treacherous slate somehow happened to slip from my hand, and falling with an obtrusive crash, directly drawn every eye upon me; I knew it was all over now, and, as I stooped to pick up the two fragments of slate, I rallied my forces for the worst. It came.

'A careless girl!' said Mr Brocklehurst, and immediately after—'It is the new pupil, I perceive.' And before I could draw breath, 'I must not forget I have a word to say respecting her.' Then aloud: how loud it seemed to me! 'Let the child who broke her slate come forward!'

Of my own accord I could not have stirred; I was paralysed: but the two great girls who sat on each side of me, set me on my legs and pushed me towards the dread judge, and then Miss Temple gently assisted me to his very feet, and I caught her whispered counsel—

'Don't be afraid, Jane, I saw it was an accident; you shall not be punished.'

'Let her stand half-an-hour longer on that stool, and let no one speak to her during the remainder of the day.'

From Jane Eyre by Charlotte Bronte

SAMPLE TEST 2

TEXT 2

Jane Fair—Scene 2: The schoolroom

Narrator	Who's this with the Head? If it isn't Mr B
	To interrupt work and interrupt tea.
	I think there's something he wants to mention.
	I was right. Here it comes …
Mr B	Aaaa … ttention!
	The laundress says each girl's -er- undies,
	are washed quite regularly on Sundays.
	That is the limit. Once a year
	Is plenty for the children here.
	And young ladies, I'd like to know
	Why lunch was served two weeks ago?
	Luncheon, luncheon?
	Whose innovation? Do you want to cause
	inflation?
Girls	Oh sir, we grow so faint and weak.
Narrator	But Mr B lets out a squeak,
	and pokes at a trembling fearful girl
	who on her forehead wears a …
Mr B	CURL! And whatismore it is red!
	The barber must shave her entire head.
Girl	But my hair is red and naturally curls.
Mr B	Nature—that is not for girls.
Narrator	All might have been well if only fate
	Had not caused Jane to drop her slate.
	It smashed in pieces and drew all eyes.
	A voice rang out
Mr B	The child who lies!
	Place her upon this chair that rebel.
	She looks like a child, but she's the devil.
Narrator	Hour after hour Jane stands alone,
	Alternatively stumbling and giving a moan.
	But don't lose heart, take some cheer,
	Jane won't be weakened by the evil here.
	She has a noble moral code
	And is determined to live for our next episode.

From *Jane Fair* © Donna Gibbs; reproduced with permission

For questions **1–8**, choose the option (**A**, **B**, **C** or **D**) which you think best answers the question.

1 Both texts are about
   A different events.   **B** similar events.
   C identical events.   **D** indistinguishable events.

2 The narrator of Text 1 is _____ in Text 2.
   A a character
   B the narrator
   C not included
   D off stage

3 In Text 1 Mr Brocklehurst shows no sign of
   A arrogance.   **B** ignorance.
   C cruelty.   **D** humility.

4 In Text 1 why does Miss Temple's voice grow quieter when speaking to Mr Brocklehurst?
   A Her throat is inflamed and getting worse.
   B She increasingly disagrees with his views.
   C She increasingly admires him.
   D She is trying to impress him with her obedience.

5 What does the author of Text 2 mainly use to satirise Text 1?
   A exaggeration
   B understatement
   C imagery
   D monologue

6 Rhyme is used in Text 2 to add to its
   A seriousness.
   B mysteriousness.
   C humour.
   D persuasiveness.

7 An important theme in both Text 1 and Text 2 is
   A hopefulness.   **B** injustice.
   C dishonesty.   **D** bravery.

8 The title of Text 2 is _____ the title of Text 1.
   A unrelated to   **B** an echo of
   C a send-up of   **D** a copy of

Read the extract below from the poem by AB 'Banjo' Paterson and then answer the questions.

Mulga Bill's Bicycle

'Twas Mulga Bill, from Eaglehawk, that caught the cycling craze;
He turned away the good old horse that served him many days;
He dressed himself in cycling clothes, resplendent to be seen;
He hurried off to town and bought a shining new machine;
And as he wheeled it through the door, with air of lordly pride,
The grinning shop assistant said, 'Excuse me, can you ride?'

'See, here, young man,' said Mulga Bill, 'from Walgett to the sea,
From Conroy's Gap to Castlereagh, there's none can ride like me.
I'm good all round at everything, as everybody knows,
Although I'm not the one to talk — I HATE a man that blows.

…

He turned the cycle down the hill and mounted for the fray,
But ere he'd gone a dozen yards it bolted clean away.
It left the track, and through the trees, just like a silver streak,
It whistled down the awful slope, towards the Dead Man's Creek.

It shaved a stump by half an inch, it dodged a big white-box:
The very wallaroos in fright went scrambling up the rocks,
The wombats hiding in their caves dug deeper underground,
As Mulga Bill, as white as chalk, sat tight to every bound.
It struck a stone and gave a spring that cleared a fallen tree,
It raced beside a precipice as close as close could be;
And then as Mulga Bill let out one last despairing shriek
It made a leap of twenty feet into the Dead Man's Creek.

'Twas Mulga Bill, from Eaglehawk, that slowly swam ashore:
He said, 'I've had some narrer shaves and lively rides before;
I've rode a wild bull round a yard to win a five pound bet,
But this was the most awful ride that I've encountered yet.
I'll give that two-wheeled outlaw best; it's shaken all my nerve
To feel it whistle through the air and plunge and buck and swerve.
It's safe at rest in Dead Man's Creek, we'll leave it lying still;
A horse's back is good enough henceforth for Mulga Bill.'

From 'Mulga Bill's Bicycle' by AB 'Banjo' Paterson

SAMPLE TEST 2

For questions **9–14**, choose the option (**A**, **B**, **C** or **D**) which you think best answers the question.

9 Mulga Bill abandoned horseriding because he
A wasn't very good at it.
B didn't want to ride a horse in the town.
C got caught up in a new craze.
D wanted to show off.

10 Which description best sums up Mulga Bill's character?
A 'a man who blows'
B shy and modest
C keen to take part in everything
D reckless

11 The bicycle is described as though it is a
A person.
B wallaroo.
C wombat.
D horse.

12 The picture created in the second-last stanza is primarily
A comical.
B tragic.
C frightening.
D bewildering.

13 The rhythm of the poem generally adds a sense of
A wandering about.
B rushing forward.
C moving stealthily.
D reflecting quietly.

14 The moral of the story is best summed up as
A never follow the latest craze.
B always tell the truth.
C pride comes before a fall.
D to thine own self be true.

SAMPLE TEST 2

Read the text then answer the questions.

Six sentences have been removed from the text. Choose from the sentences (**A–G**) the one which fits each gap (**15–20**). There is one extra sentence which you do not need to use.

Elizabeth Batts Cook (1742–1835)

Elizabeth Batts was born in 1742 in Essex, England. She was the daughter of Mary and Samuel Batts. **15** _____ He left a fortune of nine properties to his wife, Mary, who later remarried. Very little is known of Elizabeth's early life.

On 21 December 1762, Elizabeth married James Cook (1728–1799). **16** _____ Six years after their marriage James was chosen to take command of the *Endeavour*, a role which led to his fame as a navigator and explorer.

The Cooks had six children. Sadly two of these children, George and Joseph, died in infancy and their only daughter, Elizabeth, died aged four. Their son, Nathaniel, was lost during a hurricane at sea at the age of sixteen. **17** _____ Elizabeth outlived both her husband and all her children. She was married to James for seventeen years, only four of which were spent with him.

Elizabeth was a very talented embroiderer and used her skills to honour her husband's achievements. **18** _____ This is now held in the Australian National Maritime Museum collection. The map depicts various continents and countries, the equator, the tropics of Cancer and Capricorn, the Pacific, Atlantic and Southern oceans, and lines of latitude and longitude. Tiny stitches trace each of his voyages on the map.

At the time James Cook was speared to death in the Sandwich Islands, Hawaii, Elizabeth was in the process of embroidering a vest for him. **19** _____ The vest, made with tapa cloth James had brought back from his second voyage, is now in its unfinished state in the Mitchell Library, Sydney, Australia.

The sailors on Cook's last ship, the *HMS Resolution*, presented Elizabeth with a 'ditta', a sailor's carved box for personal belongings. **20** _____ Before she died, she destroyed her husband's letters in order to keep their personal relationship private.

A	She made many charitable donations in her will, including support for six poor women of her parish.
B	She planned to give it to him to wear at court after his return.
C	Her father, an innkeeper, died a few months after she was born.
D	She used it to store a tiny painting of Cook and a lock of his hair.
E	They set up home in London's East End near the Docks.
F	Their other two sons, James and Hugh, died before they had children of their own.
G	An embroidered map sampler outlines her husband's three voyages to the Pacific.

SAMPLE TEST 2

Read the four texts below on the theme of animals in danger.

For questions **21–30**, choose the option (**A**, **B**, **C** or **D**) which you think best answers the question.

Which text …

is about animals harmed by a human?	**21**	_____
reports words spoken by a conservationist?	**22**	_____
describes a successful human intervention related to the survival of a species?	**23**	_____
mentions human behaviour that, over a century ago, was endangering a species of animal?	**24**	_____
is clearly fictional?	**25**	_____
explains how a nickname came about?	**26**	_____
links modern technology with an everyday item?	**27**	_____
provides the most extreme case of an endangered species?	**28**	_____
describes a response to animal cruelty that causes personal inconvenience?	**29**	_____
explains the connection between a physical condition and increased vulnerability of a species?	**30**	_____

TEXT A

You're listening to Tom Stokes on 9SM. The news this morning is that in a village in north-eastern Kenya a white female giraffe and her calf have been found dead, slaughtered by poachers. As far as is known there is now only one white giraffe left in the world.

Their white colour is due to leucism, a rare condition that causes defects in skin cells so they are without pigmentation. Animals with this condition are left without camouflage. We know giraffe numbers have been declining but, sadly, white giraffes are now almost a thing of the past.

Conservationists in Kenya will be very keen to protect their lone remaining white giraffe. When asked what they might do, Ahmed Noor said, 'We'll fit the giraffe's horn with a GPS tracking device which will give rangers hourly updates of its whereabouts. We'll not let this one suffer the same fate as its family.' The Kenya Wildlife Society is investigating.

TEXT B

Seal Bay is on the south coast of Kangaroo Island, South Australia. It is a protected area and home to about 800 sea lions, known as 'eared' seals, a rare species with world numbers estimated at less than 12 000. The seals at Seal Bay make up the third-largest colony of the species in Australia.

Sea lions have external ear flaps, a large chest and belly (they can 'bark' loudly), and they are able to 'walk' using their four flippers. The males have short dark brown fur, although as they age it becomes tan or orange coloured around their heads and necks. They can weigh up to 400 kg. You can guess why early sailors thought of them as lions of the sea. The females are smaller than the males and have short, thick, silver hair.

During the 19th century, hunters severely reduced their numbers, driving them close to extinction. Today Australian sea lions are listed as endangered and declining.

SAMPLE TEST 2

TEXT C

There was a plowboy, Dick, who sometimes came into our field to pluck blackberries from the hedge. When he had eaten all he wanted he would have what he called fun with the colts, throwing stones and sticks at them to make them gallop. We did not much mind him, for we could gallop off; but sometimes a stone would hit and hurt us.

One day he was at this game and did not know that the master was in the next field; but he was there, watching what was going on; over the hedge he jumped in a snap, and catching Dick by the arm, he gave him such a box on the ear as made him roar with the pain and surprise. As soon as we saw the master we trotted up nearer to see what went on.

'Bad boy!' he said, 'bad boy! to chase the colts. This is not the first time, nor the second, but it shall be the last. There—take your money and go home; I shall not want you on my farm again.' So we never saw Dick any more. Old Daniel, the man who looked after the horses, was just as gentle as our master, so we were well off.

From *Black Beauty* by Anna Sewell

TEXT D

In the 1970s a frightening predator, *Euglandina rosea*, better known by its common name, rosy wolf snail, was introduced to Tahiti and other Pacific Island areas to get rid of the giant African snail. This experiment failed, as it turned out it preferred to hunt native snails. The rosy wolf snail can move at speeds of up to 30 km per hour over short distances and can climb trees. It either devours its prey whole or uses its teeth-lined 'tongue' to scrape away flesh. How did the *Partula hyaline*, a native white-shelled tree-climbing snail, survive this predator when others didn't?

Using the world's smallest computers glued to the rosy wolf snails' shells, and to leaves rested on by the *Partula hyaline*, researchers measured the light intensity of the snails' habitats. They learned that the rosy wolf snail avoided bright sunlight as it caused it to overheat but the *Partula hyaline* could tolerate hours of sunlight. They concluded solar refuges may have saved the *Partula hyaline* from extinction. If forest edge habitats are protected, they may have a fighting chance.

Read the texts below then answer the questions.

TEXT 1

The Sign of the Four

Holmes rubbed his hands, and his eyes glistened. He leaned forward in his chair with an expression of extraordinary concentration upon his clear-cut, hawklike features. 'State your case,' said he, in brisk, business tones.

…

'Briefly,' she continued, 'the facts are these. My father was an officer in an Indian regiment who sent me home when I was quite a child. My mother was dead, and I had no relative in England. I was placed, however, in a comfortable boarding establishment at Edinburgh, and there I remained until I was seventeen years of age. In the year 1878 my father, who was senior captain of his regiment, obtained twelve months' leave and came home. He telegraphed to me from London that he had arrived all safe, and directed me to come down at once, giving the Langham Hotel as his address. His message, as I remember, was full of kindness and love. On reaching London I drove to the Langham, and was informed that Captain Morstan was staying there, but that he had gone out the night before and had not yet returned. I waited all day without news of him. That night, on the advice of the manager of the hotel, I communicated with the police, and next morning we advertised in all the papers. Our inquiries led to no result; and from that day to this no word has ever been heard of my unfortunate father …'

…

'A singular case,' remarked Holmes.

'I have not yet described to you the most singular part. About six years ago—to be exact, upon the 4th of May, 1882—an advertisement appeared in the *Times* asking for the address of Miss Mary Morstan and stating that it would be to her advantage to come forward. There was no name or address appended. I had at that time just entered the family of Mrs Cecil Forrester in the capacity of governess. By her advice I published my address in the advertisement column. The same day there arrived through the post a small cardboard box addressed to me, which I found to contain a very large and lustrous pearl. No word of writing was enclosed. Since then every year upon the same date there has always appeared a similar box, containing a similar pearl, without any clue as to the sender …'

…

'This morning I received this letter, which you will perhaps read for yourself.'

'Thank you,' said Holmes. 'The envelope too, please. Postmark, London, SW. Date, July 7. Hum! Man's thumb-mark on corner,—probably postman. Best quality paper. Envelopes at sixpence a packet. Particular man in his stationery. No address. 'Be at the third pillar from the left outside the Lyceum Theatre tonight at seven o'clock. If you are distrustful, bring two friends. You are a wronged woman, and shall have justice. Do not bring police. If you do, all will be in vain. Your unknown friend.' Well, really, this is a very pretty little mystery …

From The Sign of the Four by Arthur Conan Doyle

SAMPLE TEST 3

TEXT 2

The Moonstone

The Sergeant's next proceeding was to question me (Gabriel Betteridge, in charge of the servants in the household) about any large dogs in the house who might have got into the room and done the mischief with a whisk of their tails. Hearing that this was impossible, he next sent for a magnifying-glass, and tried how the smear looked, seen that way. No skin-mark (as of a human hand) printed off on the paint. All the signs visible —signs which told that the paint had been smeared by some loose article of somebody's dress touching it in going by. That somebody (putting together Penelope's evidence and Mr. Franklin's evidence) must have been in the room, and done the mischief, between midnight and three o'clock on the Thursday morning.

Having brought his investigation to this point, Sergeant Cuff discovered that such a person as Superintendent Seegrave was still left in the room, upon which he summed up the proceedings for his brother-officer's benefit, as follows:

'This trifle of yours, Mr Superintendent,' says the Sergeant, pointing to the place on the door, 'has grown a little in importance since you noticed it last. At the present stage of the inquiry there are, as I take it, three discoveries to make, starting from that smear. Find out (first) whether there is any article of dress in this house with the smear of the paint on it. Find out (second) who that dress belongs to. Find out (third) how the person can account for having been in this room, and smeared the paint, between midnight and three in the morning. If the person can't satisfy you, you haven't far to look for the hand that has got the Diamond. I'll work this by myself, if you please, and detain you no longer from your regular business in the town.'

From *The Moonstone* by Wilkie Collins

For questions **1–8**, choose the option (**A**, **B**, **C** or **D**) which you think best answers the question.

1. Both texts are about
   A stolen jewels.
   B the nature of police work.
   C famous investigators.
   D unsolved mysteries.

2. Both investigators rely on
   A what colleagues think.
   B deduction.
   C shock tactics.
   D underhand behaviour.

3. The clue that is investigated in Text 2 relates to
   A the hairs of a dog.
   B a handprint.
   C a paint smear.
   D an article of clothing.

4. A clue that is investigated in Text 1 is
   A a thumbprint.   B a pearl.
   C a cardboard box. D a letter.

5. In which extract does the investigator show contempt for a colleague?
   A Text 1   B Text 2
   C Both   D Neither

6. In Text 1, which word does **not** apply to Miss Morstan?
   A emotional   B articulate
   C controlled   D trustworthy

7. In Text 2, which word does **not** apply to Sergeant Cuff?
   A efficient   B humble
   C thorough   D logical

8. What is the 'trifle' referred to in Text 2?
   A a reward for Cuff's colleague
   B a loose article
   C the dogs' tails brushing the wall
   D the smear of paint

SAMPLE TEST 3

Read the poem below by Sheryl Persson then answer the questions.

Horizons

In my family, I am the resident astronomer
who gazes skywards and wonders
about the pulsing universe and how it all began
my telescope is my solar system and my world
Eclipses are exciting; quasars make me quiver
I am a star-struck galaxy gazer.

My big sister, who thinks she's in control
says I should come down to earth.

Even in my dreams, I fly to distant planets
dodging meteors, comets, space junk
Then I wake up and wonder
why do we leave our rubbish in the sky
just like we pollute our earth and oceans
I tell my family it's time to act
time to save our planet and our future.

My big brother (his room is a black hole)
says I'm chasing my asteroid tail.

My mother says on cloudy nights
I moon about for light years like a solitary satellite
like Saturn without its rings
It's true—when we can't see the stars
my telescope is sad and out of orbit
and I lose my milky way.

My little brother draws a picture of a spaceship
and asks—can he come with me, deep   deep
    into   outer   space.

© Sheryl Persson; reproduced with permission

For questions **9–14**, choose the option (**A**, **B**, **C** or **D**) which you think best answers the question.

9 A 'star-struck galaxy gazer' is someone who
  A hopes to be a famous astronomer one day.
  B has an obsession with looking at things in space.
  C never stops looking into a telescope.
  D wants to visit a star sometime in the future.

10 Her big sister's attitude to the narrator's interest in astronomy is
  A critical.
  B approving.
  C indifferent.
  D admiring.

11 What makes her brother's room like 'a black hole'?
  A He has painted the walls in a dark colour.
  B What goes into it never comes out again.
  C It is hidden away under the stairs.
  D No-one can find it.

12 Why does she describe her 'way' as 'milky'?
  A The moon is shining through the stars.
  B Her telescope has turned everything white.
  C She feels lost when she can't connect with the galaxy.
  D The stars look misty.

13 The last line of the poem uses increasingly longer spaces to
  A speed up the rhythm.
  B show the poem is coming to an end.
  C prove her little brother is a dreamer.
  D create a sense of slowly entering the depths of space.

14 The poem is mainly about
  A the line where the earth meets the sky.
  B what you can see when you use a telescope.
  C different ways of seeing the world.
  D the idea that the sky is the limit.

SAMPLE TEST 3

Read the text then answer the questions.

Six sentences have been removed from the text. Choose from the sentences (**A–G**) the one which fits each gap (**15–20**). There is one extra sentence which you do not need to use.

Japanese folktales

At the turn of the last century, when the publishing houses of London and New York were market leaders in the field, Takejiro Hasegawa introduced Japanese folk tales to the West. **15** _____ The first Western readers of this cross-cultural experiment were English and French but it was not long before German, Spanish, Portuguese, Dutch and Russian readers were added to the list.

Little Peachling, the first book in the series, is a very old Japanese story about Momotaro, a boy who was born from a peach. **16** _____ He goes on adventures to fight ogres and other evils but he always returns to his parents to take care of them and give them the spoils.

This story might remind you of a popular modern tale, *James and the Giant Peach*, by Roald Dahl. **17** _____ In Dahl's tale, James has a miserable home life and escapes into a giant peach where he lives with his friends and has many adventures. In some ways it is the very opposite of Momotaro's story.

Another tale included by Hasegawa in the series is *The Boy Who Drew Cats*. A boy, the youngest of many children in his family, is clever but frail. **18** _____ He goes to live in a monastery but is expelled because all he does is draw cats! He wanders away and finds shelter in a temple but, unbeknown to him, it is the home of an evil goblin rat. **19** _____ When he wakes up, the monster is dead on the floor and traces of blood can be seen on the mouths of his cat drawings. He is hailed as a hero and goes on to become a famous artist.

These Japanese folktales are simply told and elegant but belong to an earlier era. **20** _____ Now Japanese culture reaches worldwide audiences through other art forms such as manga (Japanese comic books and graphic novels) and anime (Japanese animation).

A His parents bring him up lovingly and he grows up to be strong, brave and generous hearted.

B (The story was originally going to be about a giant cherry, but Dahl changed it to a peach because it is 'prettier, bigger and squishier than a cherry.')

C After drawing cats on some screens in a room in the temple, he goes to sleep in a nearby cupboard.

D He printed a series of volumes that used the work of western writers and translators combined with brightly coloured original woodblock prints by noted Japanese artists.

E Woodblock printing is a technique for printing text, images or patterns and has been used throughout East Asia for centuries.

F He loved to draw and from morning to evening, if you came across him anywhere, he'd probably be drawing cats.

G Books like Hasegawa's series are too time-consuming and expensive to make today.

SAMPLE TEST 3

Read the four texts below on the theme of giants.

For questions **21–30**, choose the option (**A**, **B**, **C** or **D**) which you think best answers the question.

Which text …

personifies the natural world?	21	_____
is about a friendly human being, not a 'real' giant?	22	_____
is the scariest of the giants?	23	_____
encourages people to visit unfamiliar landscapes?	24	_____
describes a giant who is most capable of feeling shame?	25	_____
is about a giant from long ago?	26	_____
is about a giant who is a bully?	27	_____
uses a metaphor to describe how a heart behaves?	28	_____
includes a giant who makes a joke?	29	_____
builds to a sudden climax?	30	_____

TEXT A

The Forgotten Giants, a group of six sculptures, can be found hidden in out-of-the-way places in Copenhagen, the modern capital city of Denmark. Thomas Dambo is the sculptor who created them. He used only recycled materials and worked with local volunteers at sites he chose carefully.

It was his idea to hide the giants in places not often visited. They are scattered about in forests, meadows and near water and there is a 31-km bike track that links them. Each giant is different. Hill Top Trine, for example, has big hands. You can climb up into them for a wonderful view of the surrounding area. Sleeping Louis, who sleeps on a hillside, has a mouth you can crawl inside. Little Tilde stands looking through the trees at a small lake. She has 28 birdhouses inside her wooden body!

TEXT B

Saul, the first king of Israel, had a restless spirit and suffered from bad dreams. In despair he appointed David, a shepherd boy and musician, to his court. Saul hoped David would be able to soothe his mind with his music.

Saul's most troublesome problem was trying to keep the Philistines under control. They had long wanted to take over Israel. Their army was made up of many exceptionally tall, strong men, including Goliath, a giant, who was over ten feet tall.

One day when the armies were assembling for battle, Goliath strode out and challenged the soldiers of Saul's army to single combat. Not a single soldier was willing to accept his offer. He repeated his challenge day after day. But David, still too young to be a soldier, was unafraid. He trusted God would protect him. Goliath laughed at the boy and then strode purposefully towards him, brandishing his sword. David took his slingshot from his belt and aimed a stone at the middle of the giant's forehead. Goliath fell dead to the ground. David was a hero and the Israelites were saved.

TEXT C

'My own garden is my own garden,' said the Giant; 'anyone can understand that, and I will allow nobody to play in it but myself.' So he built a high wall all round it and put up a notice-board: Trespassers Will be Prosecuted. He was a very selfish Giant.

…

Then the Spring came, and all over the country there were little blossoms and little birds. Only in the garden of the Selfish Giant it was still winter. The birds did not care to sing in it as there were no children and the trees forgot to blossom.

…

'I believe the Spring has come at last,' said the Giant; and he jumped out of bed and looked out. What did he see?

He saw a most wonderful sight. Through a little hole in the wall the children had crept in, and they were sitting in the branches of the trees. In every tree that he could see there was a little child. And the trees were so glad to have the children back again that they had covered themselves with blossoms and were waving their arms gently above the children's heads.

…

And the Giant's heart melted as he looked out. 'How selfish I have been!' he said; 'now I know why the Spring would not come here.

From *The Happy Prince* by Oscar Wilde

TEXT D

The *Guinness Book of Records* states that Robert Wadlow, at 2.72 metres, is the tallest man in history. Robert was born on 22 February, 1918, in Alton, Illinois, USA. By the time he was eight he was taller than his father. At 13 he joined the boy scouts and had to have a specially made uniform, tent and sleeping bag.

As a teenager he reached 2.45 metres, the tallest teenager ever. He continued to need specially made clothes and shoes (his feet were 47 cm long) as an adult. Robert was known for his kind and gentle nature, his humour and his willingness to take part in everything. When he was asked on radio if he was annoyed when people stared at him, he calmly replied, 'No, I just overlook them.'

His growth was caused by having an abnormally high level of the human growth hormone. Today this condition could be medically controlled. There are still scale models of Robert on display in different places around the world!

Read the texts below then answer the questions.

TEXT 1

My Brilliant Career

'Boo, hoo! Ow, ow; Oh! oh! Me'll die. Boo, hoo. The pain, the pain! Boo, hoo!'

'Come, come, now. Daddy's little mate isn't going to turn Turk like that, is she? I'll put some fat out of the dinner-bag on it and tie it up in my hanky. Don't cry any more now. Hush, you must not cry! You'll make old Dart buck if you kick up a row like that.'

That is my first recollection of life. I was barely three. I can remember the majestic gum-trees surrounding us, the sun glinting on their straight white trunks and falling on the gurgling fern-banked stream, which disappeared beneath a steep scrubby hill on our left. It was an hour past noon on a long clear summer day. We were on a distant part of the run, where my father had come to deposit salt. He had left home early in the dewy morning, carrying me in front of him on a little brown pillow which my mother had made for the purpose. We had put the lumps of rock-salt in the troughs on the other side of the creek. The stringybark roof of the salt-shed which protected the troughs from rain peeped out picturesquely from the musk and peppercorn shrubs by which it was densely surrounded and was visible from where we lunched. I refilled the quart-pot in which we had boiled our tea with water from the creek, father doused our fire out with it and then tied the quart to the D of his saddle with a piece of green hide.

…

'Bitey! bitey!' I yelled, and father came to my rescue, despatching the reptile with his stock-whip. He had been smoking and dropped his pipe on the ferns. I picked it up, and the glowing embers which fell from it burnt my dirty little fat fists. Hence the noise with which my story commences.

In all probability it was the burning of my fingers which so indelibly impressed the incident on my infantile mind. My father was accustomed to take me with him, but that is the only jaunt at that date which I remember, and that is all I remember of it.

…

A digging started near us and was worked by a score of two dark-browed sons of Italy. They made mother nervous, and she averred they were not to be trusted, but I liked and trusted them. They carried me on their broad shoulders, stuffed me with lollies and made a general pet of me. Without the quiver of a nerve I swung down their deepest shafts in the big bucket on the end of a rope attached to a rough windlass, which brought up the miners and the mullock.

From *My Brilliant Career* by Miles Franklin

SAMPLE TEST 4

TEXT 2

Memories of Childhood

I remember very little about the lessons because I was only seven years old, but I remember—to my inmost fibre I remember the play. There was a yard behind the house—no garden and there I used to play with another small child whose name I have forgotten. But I know that she wore a Stuart plaid frock, and that I detested her.

On the first day of my arrival we were sent into the 'playground' with our toys. Stuart plaid, as I must call her, having no other name, had a battered doll and three scallop-shells. I had a very complete little set of pewter tea-things in a cardboard box.

'Let's change for a bit,' said Stuart plaid.

Mingled politeness and shyness compelled my acquiescence. She took my new tea-things, and I disconsolately nursed the battered torso of her doll. But this grew very wearisome, and I, feeling satisfied that the claims of courtesy had been fully met, protested mildly.

'Now then,' said Stuart plaid, looking up from the tea-things …

I advanced towards her—I am afraid with some half-formed determination of pulling her hair.

'All right,' she said, 'you stand there and I'll put them in the box and give them to you.'

'Promise!'

'Yes, if you don't move.'

She turned her back on me. It took her a very long time to put them in the box. I stood tingling with indignation, and a growing desire to slap her face. Presently she turned.

'You would have them back,' she said, grinning unpleasantly, 'and here they are.'

She put them into my hands. She had bitten every single cup, saucer and plate into a formless lump!

From *Memories of Childhood* by E Nesbitt

For questions **1–8**, choose the option (**A**, **B**, **C** or **D**) which you think best answers the question.

1. Both texts are about
   A quarrelling.   B danger.
   C memories.   D promises.

2. What makes the narrator cry in Text 1?
   A being bitten by a snake
   B being burnt by hot embers
   C getting hurt at the diggings
   D getting kicked by Dart

3. Which text is set in an Australian landscape?
   A Text 1   B Text 2
   C Both   D Neither

4. In which text is emotional pain more intensely recalled than physical pain?
   A Text 1   B Text 2
   C Both   D Neither

5. In Text 1, the narrator's relationship with her father is
   A overpowering.   B distant.
   C awkward.   D close.

6. The narrators of both texts are
   A very similar to each other.
   B very different from each other.
   C about the same age.
   D from similar backgrounds.

7. In Text 2, why does the narrator refer to the girl she plays with as 'Stuart plaid'?
   A The girl insisted that was her name.
   B She was a Scottish girl.
   C She can't remember her real name.
   D She detested her.

8. In Text 2, why does Stuart plaid say 'You would have them back'?
   A to show she wants to return the tea-set
   B to deflect the blame from herself
   C to start up a new quarrel
   D to show how nasty she can be

SAMPLE TEST 4

Read the extract from the poem by DH Lawrence then answer the questions.

Snake

A snake came to my water-trough
On a hot, hot day, and I in pyjamas for the heat,
To drink there.
In the deep, strange-scented shade of the great dark
    carob-tree
I came down the steps with my pitcher
And must wait, must stand and wait, for there he
    was at the trough before me.

He reached down from a fissure in the earth-wall in
    the gloom
And trailed his yellow-brown slackness soft-bellied
    down, over the edge of the stone trough
And rested his throat upon the stone bottom,
And where the water had dripped from the tap, in a
    small clearness,
He sipped with his straight mouth,
Softly drank through his straight gums, into his
    slack long body,
Silently.
…

The voice of my education said to me
He must be killed,
For in Sicily the black, black snakes are innocent,
    the gold are venomous.
…

I looked round, I put down my pitcher,
I picked up a clumsy log
And threw it at the water-trough with a clatter.

I think it did not hit him,
But suddenly that part of him that was left behind
    convulsed in undignified haste,
Writhed like lightning, and was gone
Into the black hole, the earth-lipped fissure in the
    wall-front,
At which, in the intense still noon, I stared with
    fascination.

And immediately I regretted it.
I thought how paltry, how vulgar, what a mean act!
I despised myself and the voices of my accursed
    human education.

For questions **9–14**, choose the option (**A**, **B**, **C** or **D**) which you think best answers the question.

9 The line 'To drink there' emphasises
  A why they are at the water trough.
  B how their needs are similar.
  C the size of the water trough.
  D that it is a hot day.

10 What makes the narrator feel he 'must wait' for the snake to drink?
  A his good manners
  B a sudden impulse to stand still
  C He is afraid to move.
  D his fascination with the snake

11 The narrator throws the log at the snake because he has been taught
  A to do as he is told.
  B snakes that are venomous should always be killed.
  C snakes won't harm you if you ignore them.
  D it is unwise to harm a snake.

12 What does the narrator regret?
  A failing to hit the snake with the log
  B not getting to the trough first
  C failing to kill the snake
  D attempting to harm the snake

13 Who does the the narrator blame for his action?
  A the snake
  B himself
  C the laws in Sicily
  D the heat

14 The narrator's attitude to the snake can best be summed up as
  A terror.
  B dislike.
  C respect.
  D love.

SAMPLE TEST 4

Read the text then answer the questions.

Six sentences have been removed from the text. Choose from the sentences (**A–G**) the one which fits each gap (**15–20**). There is one extra sentence which you do not need to use.

Arnhem Land

Arnhem Land is named after the Dutch vessel *Arnhem*. **15** _____ In 1931 the area was declared an Aboriginal Reserve and officially named Arnhem Land. Arnhem Land is about 500 kilometres from Darwin, in the north-eastern corner of the Northern Territory. It covers an area of about 100 000 square kilometres. Indigenous people have lived here for tens of thousands of years. **16** _____ Many of these inhabitants are local Yolngu people, the traditional owners of the land.

Arnhem Land is Aboriginal Land and for this reason you need a permit to visit. To travel by road through Aboriginal Land, which includes the main Central Arnhem Road which connects Katherine and Nhulunbuy, you need a permit from the Northern Land Council. **17** _____ These permits are free. You may need other permits to enter recreational areas which may involve a small cost.

Much of Arnhem Land is wild and untamed. **18** _____ It has a range of natural features ranging from rivers, estuaries, tidal flats and floodplains to pristine shores, rugged coastlines and remote islands.

It has a unique history and culture that is internationally recognised. **19** _____ It is hailed as the home of the yidaki or didgeridoo. It is also home to several thousand rock art sites that rival those from sites around the world.

Art forms such as the shimmering cross-hatching or 'rarrk' technique and a style of art known as the X-ray painting style have their birthplace in Arnhem Land. The X-ray tradition has been practised there for at least 2000 years. In this style, animals and other figures are depicted in caves and rock shelters. **20** _____ Some of the images are very detailed and include parts of the body such as muscles, optic nerves and breast milk in women.

A Kakadu National Park is on the border of Arnhem Land.

B It sailed into the Gulf of Carpentaria in 1623 under the leadership of a captain of the Dutch East India Company.

C The paintings include the internal organs and bones of their subjects.

D It needs to be applied for about two weeks in advance.

E Its bark paintings from the First Nations communities of Yirrkala or Gunbalanya are currently much in demand.

F Unspoilt wilderness and stone country with rugged escarpments and magnificent ancient rainforests are part of its landscape.

G Today it has a small population of around 18 000 people.

SAMPLE TEST 4

Read the four texts below on the theme of animals' abilities.

For questions **21–30**, choose the option (**A**, **B**, **C** or **D**) which you think best answers the question.

Which extract …

describes an animal with a surprising nickname?	21	_____
discusses recent research that may lead to ridding the world of a serious problem?	22	_____
is presented in a lighthearted way?	23	_____
describes an amphibian that doesn't behave like an amphibian?	24	_____
includes the most technical language?	25	_____
explains how some researchers collect animals for their studies?	26	_____
is about an ability that can deceive?	27	_____
describes an animal's learned skill?	28	_____
is about an ability an animal can use to transform its quality of life?	29	_____
is about an ability that could help transform the planet?	30	_____

TEXT A

Did you know that your rubbish is not safe in its wheelie bin anymore? Cockatoos, especially the sulphur-crested variety, are lifting the lids and finding themselves a meal. The question of whether this behaviour is due to genetics or is a skill learned by copying others is of interest to researchers. An online survey of residents living in 478 suburbs across Sydney and Wollongong has recently been completed.

Over a two-year period, the number of sightings changed from three to 44. It was noticed that the practice was spreading more quickly across neighbouring suburbs than in random places, suggesting a learned skill. The most successful scavengers were males: their larger, stronger bodies may have helped with the tricky task.

A successful cocky would often have a group of watchers standing by. These watchers would then make their own attempts at finding a takeaway by copying what they'd seen. No-one knows how the trend started but it seems like a fine example of learning how to survive in a new environment.

TEXT B

The axolotl is often called the Mexican walking fish. It does have four legs but it is not a fish! In fact, an axolotl is the larval stage of a salamander. A salamander is an amphibian. A common pattern for an amphibian is for an egg to become a larva living in water and then to become an adult where it lives partly in water and partly on land. The axolotl doesn't follow this path. It remains in its larval form. It lives permanently in water and breathes through its gills and skin, although it also has lungs.

One of their remarkable skills is that they can regenerate lost body parts and can rebuild parts of their own jaws, spines and even brains without creating scar tissue. Scientists continue to study the axolotl in their laboratories. Many are bred in captivity for this purpose. The wild axolotl is now an endangered species.

TEXT C

The superb lyrebird is native to Australia and lives in forests to the west of the Great Dividing Range. Fossils held in the Australian Museum show lyrebirds lived in Australia as far back as 15 million years ago.

Superb lyrebirds have strong legs with long toes and claws. Their wings are small and not strongly muscled. They are famous mimics. They don't only copy sounds made by other birds and animals but often imitate sounds made by a train, a chainsaw, a car engine or even a mobile phone! Researchers have found evidence that their mimicry is so accurate that an imitated species can't distinguish between the lyrebird's sounds and those made by their own species.

Courtship offers another chance for the male to 'sing'. He raises his long colourful tail feathers in a spectacular show then courts his smaller, less showy mate.

TEXT D

Researchers at Brandon University in Manitoba, Canada, have recently discovered a species of caterpillar that may help the world with its plastic disposal problem. Each year millions of tons of plastic go to waste, causing havoc on land and at sea.

The species of caterpillar that offers some hope is the waxworm. It is able to eat through many types of plastic including polyethylene, a nonbiodegradable type of plastic of the kind used in plastic bags. Researchers have found that the waxworm has microorganisms in its gut that enables it to eat and metabolise plastics into biodegradable products at extraordinary speeds.

More needs to be discovered about how the waxworm and its gut bacteria work together and ways found to use this new knowledge. As Dr Bryan Cassone says, 'Once we figure this out, we can use the information to design better tools to eliminate plastics from our environment.'

1 On an excursion, 25 students bought ice creams at an ice-cream parlour. They had the choice of single, double or triple scoop ice-cream cones. In total, 47 scoops of ice cream were served. If 12 students ordered single scoops, how many students ordered double scoops?

A 0   **B** 4   **C** 8   **D** 13

2 Cassowaries don't swim for pleasure but they will swim when they need to, such as when trying to avoid a pack of wild dogs.

Katy: 'That bird over there is swimming. There aren't any dogs around. It can't be a cassowary.'

Daniel: 'Perhaps it's a cassowary that needed to swim to get to the other side of the river.'

If the information in the box is true, whose reasoning is correct?

A Katy only

B Daniel only

C Both Katy and Daniel

D Neither Katy nor Daniel

3 Margaret wanted to build a bench around the base of one of her four trees so she could sit in her garden. She decided to build it around the tree that was growing the slowest so she wouldn't have to pull out her bench any time soon.

- The Jacaranda had been planted at 1m tall 9 years ago and was now 4.6 m tall.

- The Spotted Gum had been planted at 1.4 m tall 3 years ago and was now 2.9 m tall.

- The Paper Bark had been grown from a seed 5 years ago and was now 2.5 m tall.

- The Camphor Laurel was already 2.2 m tall when Margaret bought the house 10 years ago and was now 7.7 m tall.

Which tree should she build her bench around?

A The Jacaranda

B The Spotted Gum

C The Paper Bark

D The Camphor Laurel

4 Three runners completed the 100-m sprint. Alec beat Thomas by 10 m. Thomas in turn beat Christo by 10 m.

If the runners ran at a constant speed for the entire race, by how many metres did Alec beat Christo?

A 19 m   **B** 20 m   **C** 21 m   **D** 22 m

5 Freya has written a letter to the local council. She has suggested that, to support the council's zero-waste target, the council should implement a household food scraps recycling program across the community.

Which one of these statements, if true, most **strengthens** Freya's argument?

A The food scraps will be converted to green electricity and fertiliser.

B Collecting and recycling food waste is a positive step to help mitigate climate change.

C Food scraps typically make up one third of household waste that ends up in landfill.

D The council needs to implement programs to help it reach its zero-waste target.

6 Four pieces are needed to make the 4-by-4 square pictured:

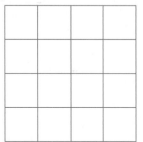

SAMPLE TEST 1

Hannah has the first piece:

Which other three pieces will **not** make the square?

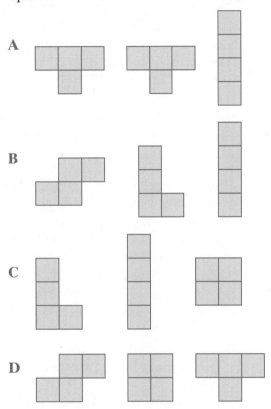

A

B

C

D

---

7 Tayla, Brenda and Tom started their school day with the same number of trading cards. While playing with other students, Tayla won an extra eight cards, Brenda won an extra 25 and Tom lost 13 cards. They now have 65 cards between them.

How many cards did each student start the day with?

A 10   **B** 15   **C** 20   **D** 25

---

8 If David does not practise his goal kicking, then his ability to kick goals won't improve.

If his ability to kick goals doesn't improve, he might not be able to successfully kick a goal when necessary in the finals match in two weeks. If he does not kick a goal when required then his team might lose the match. Improved goal kicking will improve his team's chance of winning.

Based on the above information, which one of the following **cannot** be true?

A David didn't practise but his goal kicking improved.

B David didn't practise but his team still won.

C David practised every day but his team did not win.

D David practised but his penalty kicking did not improve.

---

9 Legumes are foods that grow in pods, such as peas, beans and lentils. Pulses are the dried seeds of legume plants. Pulses include chickpeas, lentils, kidney beans, black beans and butter beans. You have to cook pulses before eating them. The most popular legume in Australia is the chickpea. People use it to make hummus.

If this is true, which one of these sentences must also be true?

A Chickpeas are popular legumes in Australia because people like hummus.

B Hummus is made from dried peas, beans and lentils.

C Pulses are dried seeds of legume plants that require no cooking before eating.

D Hummus is made from cooked chickpeas.

---

10 In the Wimbledon Ladies singles tennis competition, 128 players compete in 64 separate matches in Round 1. After the first round, half the competitors are knocked out and the other half play in Round 2. This continues until the final two players face off in the final. If the Gentlemen's competition runs the same way, how many singles matches are played at Wimbledon over both competitions?

A 63   **B** 127   **C** 254   **D** 256

11 When Hans tried out for the soccer team he was told that he could start out as reserve goalie and would be allowed to play for some time during the second half of matches where the team was in a winning position; that is, in any game where the team is two goals ahead of the opposition at half-time and remained two goals ahead. He would not get any game time if the team was losing because they would need to keep their best goalie on the field.

Which one of the following sentences must be true?

A In a match where the score was 3–1 in favour of Hans's team, he would be allowed on the field for the first half of the match only.

B In a match where the score was 0–0, Hans would only be allowed to play for the final quarter of the game.

C In a match where the score was 2–0, Hans would be allowed on the field as goalie for some time in the second half.

D In a match where the score was 4–2, Hans would be allowed to play for some time in the second half but not as goalie.

12 Shown below are the three small pieces of a puzzle:

Which one of the following big pieces can be combined with the three small pieces to make a square?

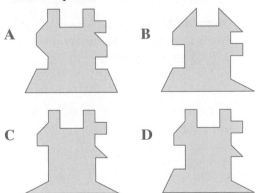

13 For the following question, shapes that are reflections or rotations of each other are considered the same shape. For example:

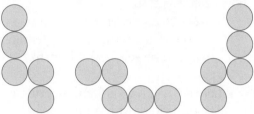

are the same shape.

The following shape can be transformed into three other shapes by moving only one of the small circles to another position:

For which shape is this **not** possible?

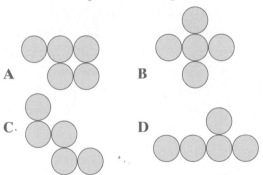

14 The sports teacher told Zara's class that any students who were not selected for the volleyball team last term will definitely be given a chance to try out for selection this term as there will be two teams in future, rather than one.

Which one of the following shows **incorrect** reasoning?

A **Toni:** 'Marcus tried out but missed selection last term so he will have a greater chance of being selected this term.'

B **Veronica:** 'Just because Marcus was not selected last term and he'll be given a chance to try out this term, it does not mean he will be selected.'

C Leo: 'Just because Marcus will be given a chance to try out for selection this term, it does not mean he'll want to try out this term.'

D Bec: 'Because Marcus did not get selected last term, he will definitely want to be selected this term.'

15 **Lauren:** 'I have an 8 am meeting in the city on Friday with a new client.'
Tobias: 'You'd better catch the 5 am bus then to allow plenty of time to get there.'

Which one of the following sentences shows the mistake Tobias has made?

A The meeting is important to Lauren.

B Lauren works in the city.

C Lauren is catching an early bus to work.

D Lauren is catching the bus because she does not have a car.

16 Carlo wanted to tile his bathroom floor with hexagonal tiles. He chose the following pattern:

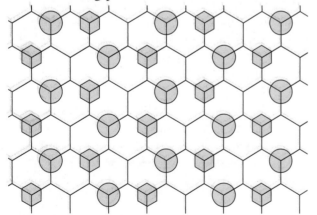

How many distinct tile designs does Carlo need to buy?

A 1   B 2   C 3   D 6

17 Alejandro says, 'I know it's against the law for a pedestrian to cross a road against a flashing red light but I've never seen or heard of anyone getting caught and fined so I'm going to cross against this flashing light.'

Based on the above information, which one of the following **cannot** be true?

A It's against the law for a pedestrian to cross a road against a flashing red light.

B Police catch people who break the law.

C Alejandro has never seen or heard of anyone getting caught and fined.

D If you've never seen or heard of anyone getting caught, it's ok to cross against a flashing red light.

18 To have a chance of success at competitive indoor rock climbing you need fitness and flexibility, a strong core, and strong fingers and arms. You also need good problem-solving skills because you have to climb a wall along a route set by a route setter that you won't have seen before and you'll only be given one chance to do it and get as high on the route as you can.

Duncan: 'Keegan trains hard and sets practice goals to constantly improve her skills. She is determined to be a successful rock-climbing competitor. She's fit and strong and a good problem solver. She'll do everything she can to win. I know she will achieve her goals.'

Myumi: 'Ed is mentally tough and a great problem solver. He works hard at increasing his strength and fitness but he struggles with finger strength and has had a number of finger injuries or pulley strains. He has to tape a number of his fingers to support them. He has a great attitude though and that will give him a good chance of success.'

If the information in the box is true, whose reasoning is correct?

A Duncan only

B Myumi only

C Both Duncan and Myumi

D Neither Duncan nor Myumi

19 On an analog clock, the hour hand completes a full revolution every 12 hours. The minute hand completes a full revolution every hour. How many times will the minute hand point in the exact same direction as the hour hand in a single day?

A 11   B 12   C 22   D 24

20 Elderly people in aged care require physical and mental exercise and social interaction for optimum wellbeing. Aged-care homes should provide opportunities for residents to engage in a variety of activities to keep them active and alert. Activities should be aimed at preserving people's physical abilities and skills, memory, independence and dignity. People can be supported to continue hobbies or take up new hobbies.

Which statement best expresses the main idea of the text?

A Activities can be designed to preserve people's physical abilities and skills, memory, independence and dignity.

B For optimum wellbeing, elderly people require physical and mental exercise and social interaction.

C Aged-care residents need to engage in a variety of activities.

D Continuing hobbies or taking up new hobbies benefits the wellbeing of the elderly.

21 Ilya surveyed class members to find out which kinds of movies would be most popular if he hosted a movie marathon night at his place. He found that:

- everyone who enjoys scary movies/ thrillers likes action/adventure movies.

- everyone who enjoys action/adventure movies likes science-fiction movies.

- no-one who enjoys action/adventure movies likes comedies.

His four best friends in the class—Nadia, Twyla, Daniel and David—answered the survey.

Based on the above information, which one of the following must be true?

A If Nadia enjoys science-fiction movies, she also enjoys action/adventure movies.

B If David does not like comedy, he does not like science fiction.

C If Twyla likes scary movies and thrillers, she does not enjoy comedy.

D If Daniel does not enjoy scary movies or thrillers, he does not like action/ adventure movies.

22 Five children are part of the same family. Callan is one year older than Olive. Ned is five years older than Molly. Callan is five years younger than Isla. Molly is two years younger than Olive.

If Olive is nine years old, which of the following is also true?

A Ned is 13.

B Isla is 15.

C Callan is the second-oldest child.

D Ned is the oldest child.

23 When viewed from above, an object looks like the picture shown below:

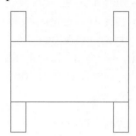

Which one of the following is **not** a possible view from the side?

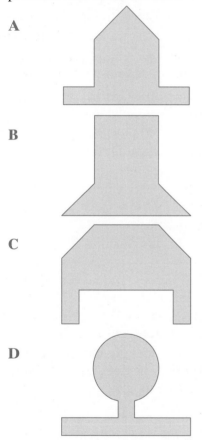

A

B

C

D

24 Landcare is one of the largest volunteer movements in Australia. It involves a diverse range of people in communities across the country working towards a balance between sustainable land use and environmental conservation. Landcare is not just good for the environment; it's also good for building cohesive communities.

Which one of the following, if true, most **strengthens** the above argument?

A Children can become involved in caring for the land by joining Landcare Junior.

B Landcare works on natural habitat restoration in order to enhance biodiversity.

C Due to climate change and natural disasters, the work of Landcare volunteers is more important now than ever.

D Landcare became a national program in 1989 with support from the Australian Government.

25 In one country it is custom for a first son to be named after the father's father and for the second son to be named after the mother's father. The third son then receives a different name. A grandfather has five daughters and two sons.

- His first daughter had three sons and one daughter.
- His second daughter had two sons.
- His third daughter had two sons and one daughter.
- His fourth daughter had two sons.
- His fifth daughter had two daughters.
- His first son had one son.
- His second son had no children.

How many male grandchildren had the same name as the grandfather?

A 5   B 3   C 6   D 4

26 Terminology makes a huge difference to perception. In Sydney, prior to the 1930s, incidents where a shark bit a human were referred to as 'shark accidents'. Scientists and conservationists prefer the media to use the phrase 'shark bite' instead of 'shark attack' when reporting these kinds of shark encounters.

Which one of these statements, if true, most **weakens** the above argument?

A Any encounter with a shark that leaves teeth marks is an attack.

B Sharks don't attack people with a view to eating them.

C More than a third of shark encounters leave no injury or leave only small bite marks.

D Sharks might attempt to bite a human just to see if it is food.

27 Which is the shortest combination of sentences that, if true, prove that Ned is a good dog?

1. All good dogs chase their tail.
2. Ned chases his tail.
3. All good dogs sit when they are told to.
4. Ned sits when he is told to.
5. All dogs that chase their tail are good dogs.

A 1 and 2   B 3 and 4
C 2 and 5   D 1, 2 and 5

28 After four days in the sun, I learnt a valuable lesson about skincare. I learnt that when I put multiple layers of sunscreen on, I don't get sunburnt.

I logged my activity and the results in the table below:

day	Did I apply multiple layers of sunscreen?	Did I get sunburnt?
1	no	(a)
2	(b)	yes
3	yes	(c)
4	(d)	no

Which **two** of the missing answers **must** be known in order to test the truth of the valuable lesson I learnt?

A **a** and **b**   B **b** and **d**
C **a** and **c**   D **b** and **c**

29 Behind three doors two deadly creatures lie in wait. A venomous snake lies behind one door and a tiger lies behind another. Only one door leads to safety. On each door are written two statements. However, only three of the six statements are true.

Door 1	Door 2	Door 3
The tiger is not here.	The tiger is behind Door 1.	The tiger is here.
The snake is not here.	The snake is behind Door 3.	The snake is behind Door 2.

Which **one** of the following statements **cannot** be true?

A The tiger is behind Door 1 and the snake is behind Door 3.

B The tiger is behind Door 2 and Door 1 leads to safety.

C The snake is behind Door 2.

D The tiger is behind Door 3.

30 The main street of a small city includes five buildings all situated in a row. Each building is home to one business.

- The bank is immediately to the left of the sporting-goods store.
- The sporting-goods store is two storeys high.
- The music store is immediately to the right of the bookstore.
- The music store is one storey high.
- The buildings at the two ends of the row are the same height.
- The medical practice has twice as many storeys as the sporting-goods store and is on the far right of the row.
- The music store and the bookstore together have as many storeys as the bank.

If the bank is in the middle of the row, how many storeys does the bookstore have?

A 2   B 3   C 4   D 5

31 Anika is building a cabinet for her woodwork project. The best cabinet will win the Woodwork Prize at the end of the year.

- If Anika takes her time when measuring, it is likely she will make no large mistakes.
- If she makes any large mistakes, she will not construct a good-quality cabinet.
- If she makes a good-quality cabinet, she has a good chance of securing the Woodwork Prize.
- If she does not, then she has no chance at all.

If all the above statements are true, only **one** of the sentences below **cannot** be true. Which one?

A Anika made a large mistake but still won the prize.

B Anika took her time when measuring but did not win the prize.

C Anika made no mistakes but didn't win the prize.

D Anika didn't take her time when measuring but still made a good-quality cabinet.

32 A group of students was asked which board games they like to play. The following information was gathered.

- All those who like draughts also like chess.
- All those who like Yahtzee like backgammon.
- Some of those who like draughts also like backgammon.
- None who like Yahtzee like draughts.

Which of the following statements **cannot** be true?

A All who like Yahtzee like chess.

B None who like chess like Yahtzee.

C All who like backgammon like chess.

D None who like backgammon like chess.

33 There are two ways to earn a free smoothie at Juice Meadow. You can download the Juice Meadow App and be rewarded with five, first-time customer loyalty credits to exchange for a free smoothie. Or you can earn one free smoothie for every five smoothies purchased.

If the information in the box is true, whose reasoning is correct?

A **Abby:** 'I know that six students in my class can get a free smoothie today. So they must have downloaded the App.'

B **Samantha:** 'If you download the App twice, you can get two free smoothies.'

C **Jordan:** 'Every free smoothie earns one store credit.'

D **Lucy:** 'Ten smoothie purchases earn two free smoothies.'

34 If you plant garlic on the shortest day of the year and harvest it on the longest day of the year, your garlic bulbs will be both large and flavoursome.

Two keen gardeners were discussing the garlic they had purchased from a grocery store.

Gary: 'This garlic is neither large nor flavoursome so it mustn't have been planted on the shortest day of the year.'

Rani: 'This garlic is neither large nor flavoursome so it mustn't have been harvested on the longest day of the year.'

If the information in the box is true, whose reasoning is correct?

A Gary only

B Rani only

C Both Gary and Rani

D Neither Gary nor Rani

35 Raphael said, 'You can't call yourself an animal lover if you would ever condone killing an animal. Killing animals is cruel and unnecessary.'

Which one of these statements, if true, most **weakens** Raphael's argument?

A As well as being cruel, hunting has contributed to animal extinctions throughout history.

B There are some circumstances where you need to put an animal down because you don't want it to suffer.

C There are ways to control feral animals that don't involve killing them inhumanely.

D If you love animals, you will cut back on your consumption of meat.

36 Three Olympic skateboarders discussed their chances in the final.

Pedro: 'If I land every trick, I will win a medal.'

Keegan: 'If I don't skate at my best, I will not win a medal.'

Rune: 'If I fall off my board, I will retire after the competition.'

Pedro won gold, Keegan won silver and Rune retired after the competition.

If all the above statements are true, what else must be true?

A Pedro landed every trick.

B Keegan skated at his best.

C Rune fell off his board.

D all of the above

37 'A successful restaurant must have good customer service and serve tasty food.'

If this is true, which one of these sentences must also be true?

A Millie's Restaurant has good customer service and serves tasty food so it must be successful.

B If Millie's Restaurant is not successful, it cannot serve tasty food.

C If Millie's Restaurant is not successful, it cannot have good customer service.

D If Millie's Restaurant has bad customer service, it cannot be successful.

38 **Blake:** 'If you don't get enough protein in your diet, you will be unhealthy. Vegetarians don't eat meat so they must be unhealthy.'

Which one of the following sentences shows the mistake Blake has made?

A Eating meat is the only way people can get protein in their diet.

B If you don't eat meat, you can't be healthy.

C Lentils are a good source of protein.

D Vegetarians are unhealthy.

39 **Satoko:** 'Pumpkin is one of my favourite vegetables. It makes sweet or savoury dishes including pumpkin pie or pancakes, pumpkin chocolate brownies, pumpkin soup, roast pumpkin, pumpkin risotto, tarts and quiches and it is even delicious when roasted and added to a salad. Pumpkin is a very versatile vegetable.'

Which statement best expresses Satoko's main idea?

A Pumpkin is one of Satoko's favourite vegetables.

B Pumpkin can be used in pies and tarts and soup.

C Pumpkin is a very versatile vegetable.

D People all over the world eat pumpkin.

40 Five sprinters are the only competitors in a 100-m race. The following is known:

• Jennifer is faster than Marion.

• Isabella is faster than Simone.

• Marion is faster than Simone.

• Cathy is faster than Isabella.

Which statement **cannot** be true?

A Jennifer wins the race.

B Cathy wins the race.

C Simone comes fourth.

D Isabella comes fourth.

1 Look at the diagram below:

The cog at the top left is turned in the direction of the black arrow.

What will happen to the four weights?

A 1 and 3 will go up; 2 and 4 will go down.

B 1 and 3 will go down; 2 and 4 will go up.

C 1 and 4 will go up; 2 and 3 will go down.

D 1 and 4 will go down; 2 and 3 will go up.

2 Imogen's netball club has qualified for the finals with both its A and B teams. Imogen was told that to be eligible to play in a finals game she must have played a minimum of six home or away games for the club. Imogen usually plays in the B team but for seven of the twelve games this season she has been asked to play in the A team. Any player who has played half or more of the possible home and away games with teams in higher grades will not be allowed to play in finals games in a lower grade. Imogen wants to play in the competition finals game with the B team.

If the information above is true, only one of the sentences below **cannot** be true. Which one?

A Imogen will not be allowed to play in the finals for the B team.

B Imogen has qualified for the competition finals.

C Imogen has qualified to play in the A-team finals game.

D Imogen has qualified to play in the B-team finals game.

3 A standard six-sided dice has opposite sides adding to 7. Using this information, which of the following is **not** a possible view of a standard six-sided dice?

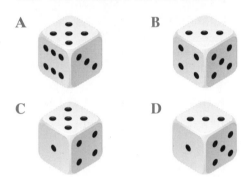

4 The Broken Hill Bridge Club meets every Sunday and Monday. They also meet on the first, third and fifth Thursday of every month. They don't play on Christmas Day (25 December), Boxing Day (26 December) or New Year's Day (1 January).

If 1 December 2022 is a Thursday, on how many days do they meet in December 2022 and January 2023?

A 20   **B** 21   **C** 22   **D** 23

5 Cleopatra was the last pharaoh of Egypt. She was a strong and powerful ruler in a male-dominated era. She studied and used her intellect to consolidate her rule and to protect her empire. She was a strategist and built alliances with powerful men, such as Julius Caesar and Marc Antony, to help protect her empire from invasion. She managed to keep Egypt independent and safe during tumultuous times.

Which statement best expresses the main idea of the text?

A Cleopatra was the last pharaoh of Egypt.

B Cleopatra was a strong and powerful ruler in a male-dominated era.

C Cleopatra was a strategist who built alliances with powerful men.

D Cleopatra managed to keep Egypt independent and safe during tumultuous times.

6 In a zoo on a distant planet, Dini counted 20 animals in a particular enclosure. This enclosure contained three species of animal: plinkers, blippos and glizzos.

Dini noticed the following:

• Plinkers have four legs.

• Blippos have two legs.

• There were five glizzos.

• There was one more plinker than blippo.

• There were 76 legs altogether.

How many legs does a glizzo have?

A 2   B 5   C 6   D 8

7 Aaron sets out for a walk. He starts by walking 1 km north from his starting position. He then heads east for 1 km. After this he walks 2 km south before walking 2 km west. He decides to continue to walk north, then east, then south, then west, increasing the distance by 1 km every two changes of direction. So he now turns and walks 3 km north. After walking 33 km in total, Aaron decides to return straight back to his starting position.

How far does he need to walk and in which direction must he travel?

A 2 km heading east

B 3 km heading east

C 3 km heading west

D 3 km heading south

8 Year 6 students did a survey of children in lower primary to find out which colour they'd like to have their new playground cubby house painted. They found the following:

• Children preferred yellow to blue.

• Children liked purple less than they liked yellow.

• Children preferred green to orange.

• Children liked green less than purple.

• Red and purple were equally popular.

Based on the above information, which one of the following must be true?

A The cubby house will be painted purple and red.

B The cubby house will be painted blue.

C The cubby house will be painted yellow.

D The cubby house will be painted green.

9 Collisions and entanglements with wire fences and especially barbed-wire fences cause horrific injuries or painful deaths to wildlife. According to WIRES (the Wildlife Information, Rescue and Education Service), over 75 different species including flying foxes, owls, kangaroos and emus are on record as victims of a wire fence injury.

Which one of these statements, if true, most **weakens** the argument in the box?

A Barbed wire deters livestock from rubbing against a fence and damaging it.

B Use wildlife-friendly alternatives to wire fences.

C Avoid using barbed-wire near feed trees or across wildlife corridors.

D Increase the visibility of a wire fence by using white nylon sighter wires or cover any barbed wire near feeder trees or shrubs with white polypipe.

10 In the game of Yahtzee, five regular six-sided dice are rolled.

- If two dice land on the same number, it is said to be a pair.
- If three dice land on the same number, it is said to be three of a kind.
- If you roll a pair and three of a kind on the same roll, you are said to have a full house.

Terrence rolled a full house. The sum of all five dice is found to be an odd number. Which of the following statements **cannot** be true?

A Terrence has three of a kind of an odd number.

B Terrence scored 21 and the dice showed at least two 6s.

C The difference between the sum of the pair and the sum of the three of a kind is 1.

D Terrence scored 19 and has no 5s.

11

Good nurses show empathy, compassion and respect to their patients in a person-centred approach to health care. They also have excellent communication skills.

Aran: 'Gabriella has a caring attitude towards all of her friends. She offers to bring them soup if they have a cold. Also she is very respectful of her grandparents. I know she has excellent communication skills because she wants to be a writer. She will make an excellent nurse.'

Nikita: 'Nazeem is kind and compassionate to others and has excellent communication skills so he has all the qualities listed that would make him a good nurse. He faints at the sight of blood but I'm sure he would readily overcome that phobia. He will make a great nurse.'

Based on the information in the box, whose reasoning is correct?

A Aran only

B Nikita only

C Neither Aran nor Nikita

D Both Aran and Nikita

12 A standard deck of 52 playing cards is split into four suits: hearts, spades, diamonds and clubs. Each suit has 13 cards. If a standard deck is shuffled and completely dealt out to four players so each has the same number of cards, which must be true?

A All players have at least one heart.

B Some players have no spades.

C No player has all the hearts.

D One player has at least four spades.

13 Shown below are the three small pieces of a puzzle:

Which one of the following big pieces can be combined with the three small pieces to make a square?

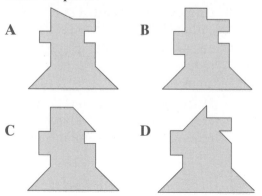

A   B

C   D

14 'Whoever untied the dog from the fence at the park and took it to the animal shelter must have had both the time and a good reason.'

If this is true, which one of these sentences must also be true?

A If Yvette had both the time and a good reason, she must have taken the dog.

B If Yvette did not have a good reason to take the dog, she cannot have taken it.

C If Yvette did not take the dog, she cannot have had the time.

D If Yvette did not take the dog, she cannot have had a good reason.

15 Eli researched farming and climate change. He presented his findings in a speech to the class:

"Fifty-one per cent of land in Australia is used for farming. Farmers understand that agriculture is particularly vulnerable to climate change and that the way they farm can help mitigate climate change. Across the planet, farmers are working with governments, scientists, their local communities and their own farming networks to reduce emissions and become carbon neutral or carbon negative.'

Which one of these statements, if true, most **strengthens** Eli's argument?

A Farmers are playing a vital role in ensuring resilience to climate change in rural areas.

B Farmers have adapted practices to store carbon, including in the soil.

C Technologies are being adopted to reduce methane emissions from grazing animals.

D Hydrogen-powered tractors mean that diesel and petrol will no longer be required to power farm machinery.

16 Two young friends live across the road from each other and have developed a way of communicating from their bedrooms after dark. The friends both have a window with four panes of glass and both own two torches. At night they place torches in the windowpanes to send messages.

No torches means 'I'm asleep.'

The window on the right means 'Let's ride our bikes to school tomorrow':

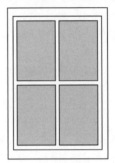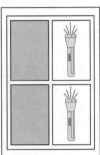

Only one torch can be in each pane. Counting the two already shown, how many different messages can the friends send each other?

A 8   B 9   C 10   D 11

17 **Mariah:** 'I'm feeling lucky today. I've bought twenty lottery tickets instead of my usual one. I'm sure to win a prize with that many tickets. I'm going to buy a new car with my winnings.'

Which one of the following sentences shows the mistake Mariah has made?

A Mariah feels lucky.

B Mariah cannot be certain she will win.

C Buying extra tickets increases your chance of winning.

D Mariah is planning how to spend her money before she has even won it.

18 Animals can sense when an earthquake is going to occur. Scientists in an earthquake-prone area of Italy attached sensors to cows, sheep and dogs and monitored their movements. They found the animals became increasingly restless up to 20 hours before an earthquake and were even more restless the closer they were to the epicentre of the earthquake. Scientists think that animals might smell the gases released before an earthquake or may sense the ionisation of the air or minor early trembles within the earth.

Reggie said: 'My dog is unusually restless this afternoon. We might be about to experience an earthquake.'

Brett: 'The research is interesting but other factors could explain the behaviour of Reggie's dog. Reggie is wrong to claim his dog can predict an earthquake.'

Carly: 'I accept the possibility that animals can sense all sorts of things including an earthquake but I don't think Reggie can say his dog is restless because it senses an earthquake is coming.'

If the information in the box is true, whose reasoning is correct?

A Brett only

B Carly only

C Both Brett and Carly

D Neither Brett nor Carly

19 Martha was sent to the shops by her mother to buy as many pizzas as she could. The shop had a number of deals on and they are shown below:

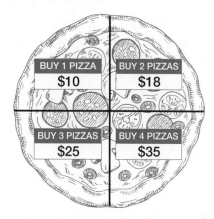

BUY 1 PIZZA $10   BUY 2 PIZZAS $18

BUY 3 PIZZAS $25   BUY 4 PIZZAS $35

Martha was given $80 and was told she could keep the change, once she had bought as many pizzas as she could afford.

What is the maximum amount that Martha can keep?

A $0   B $2   C $5   D $8

20 A community radio station is giving away free passes to the music festival in July. There are two ways to win a free pass: either by phoning the station and correctly answering at least five out of ten music trivia questions or by submitting a self-recorded original piece of music.

Viktor: 'Ten people I know have received a free pass to the festival. I know two of them answered nine questions correctly, two answered five questions correctly and one answered six questions correctly so that means five of them have won a free pass for a self-recorded original piece of music.'

SAMPLE TEST 2

Which one of the following sentences shows the mistake Viktor has made?

A The radio station might hve been allowed to give away more than ten free passes.

B Some of the winners might have earned a prize even if they did not answer more than five questions correctly or self-record an original piece of music or song.

C No-one who won a free pass answered more than five questions correctly.

D There may be other ways to win a free pass to the festival.

21 Conspiracy theories have always had their followers and social media allows conspiracy theory propaganda to reach larger audiences. Proponents of conspiracy theories think scientists and governments conspire to lie to people. One conspiracy theory is that the Earth is flat. Flat-earthers think the Earth is flat in spite of the fact we have known the Earth is a sphere since at least 322 BC when the Greek Philosopher Aristotle travelled from Greece to Egypt. Aristotle had noticed that the night sky over Egypt revealed different constellations of stars than those he could see from Greece. Images of Earth taken from space should be enough proof for anyone that the Earth is a sphere but flat-earthers believe these photos are a conspiracy too. Many flat-earthers don't even believe there was a moon landing. They think the film footage was fake.

Based on the above information, which one of the following statements **cannot** be true?

A Conspiracy theorists are always prepared to change their minds if they are shown evidence.

B Conspiracy theorists have a deep mistrust of the government and institutions.

C Conspiracy theorists have lost the ability to judge for themselves whether something is true or a conspiracy.

D Conspiracy theorists believe what they read on social media more than they believe scientists or doctors.

22 In an effort to get fit, Kristina set herself a seven-day challenge. On Monday she completed a number of push-ups. On Tuesday she completed one more push-up than she did on Monday. On Wednesday she completed two more push-ups than she did on Tuesday. On Thursday she completed three more push-ups than she did on Wednesday. This pattern continued to Sunday.

If she completed 36 push-ups on Sunday, how many push-ups did she complete on Monday?

A 5   B 15   C 25   D 30

23 Sean and Takuma have been work colleagues for two years and usually have a good working relationship but lately Takuma has noticed that Sean is very short-tempered with him. Takuma decides to avoid Sean.

What is Takuma's assumption?

A Sean is unhappy.

B He must be the cause of Sean's short temper.

C Sean is unfriendly.

D Sean is more short-tempered lately.

24 Fifty-two artworks were submitted to a gallery for an exhibition. Artists were allowed to submit a maximum of four artworks each.

If four times as many artists entered one artwork than entered three artworks and four times as many artists entered three artworks than entered four artworks, how many people submitted two artworks to the gallery?

A 10   B 12   C 14   D 16

25 One worker can make 24 products in an hour and another can make 36 of the same products in an hour. How long would it take them to make 25 products if they worked together?

A 25 minutes

B 30 minutes

C 35 minutes

D 40 minutes

26 A number of children at Scarlet's school have an allergy to peanuts. The school has a 'no peanut and no peanut butter' policy and any peanut items are prohibited from school. The school fete is coming up at the end of the month and the fete coordinators have decided to allow the sale of peanut-butter cookies and other peanut items as long as they are clearly labelled as containing peanuts. The fete coordinators believe that since the main aim of the fete is to raise funds for the school, restricting the sale of peanut products will reduce the fete's profitability.

Scarlet disagrees with the fete coordinators. She argues that because peanut products are not allowed at school, they should not be sold at the fete.

Which one of the following, if true, most **strengthens** Scarlet's argument?

A Food allergies are a growing safety concern that affect any number of people in the community.

B The school must ensure the health and safety of its students and put student wellbeing ahead of profits.

C Children from the school will attend the fete and many of them like peanut-butter cookies.

D It would be hypocritical to sell peanut products at the fete when those same products are prohibited at school.

27 Which is the shortest combination of sentences that, if true, prove that Eva is an elite athlete?

1. Eva regularly finishes in the top 10 of national competitions.

2. Eva trains for more than 15 hours every week.

3. All elite athletes train for more than 15 hours every week.

4. Athletes are considered elite if they consistently finish in the top 20 in national competitions.

A 1 and 2

B 1 and 4

C 2 and 3

D 1, 2, 3, and 4

28 A garden supplies company was marketing a new lawn fertiliser. It claimed that 'LUSH LAWN will make your lawn grow thick and lush'.

Four lawns were monitored to check the truth of the claim:

lawn	Was LUSH LAWN used?	Is the lawn thick and lush?
1	(a)	yes
2	yes	(b)
3	(c)	no
4	no	(d)

Which two of the missing answers must be known in order to test the truth of the claim?

A **a** and **b**

B **b** and **c**

C **c** and **d**

D **a** and **d**

29 Maggie is babysitting the three Chan children: David, Jason and Olivia. She hears a crash from the lounge room and finds the three children standing around a broken glass table. She asked them who broke it and they responded like this:

David: 'I didn't do it. Jason did it.'

Jason: 'David is telling a lie. Olivia did it.'

Olivia: 'I didn't do it. Jason did it.'

Before leaving, Mrs Chan had told her one child always lies, one always tells the truth and another will always tell a truth and a lie. The problem is that Maggie can't remember which child does what.

Who broke the table?

A David

B Jason

C Olivia

D There is not enough information to decide.

30 If Hima doesn't warm up, she is likely to injure herself.

If Hima injures herself, she will not train well.

If Hima trains well, she is likely to win the 100-m sprint.

If she doesn't train well, she has no chance.

If the above statements are correct, which one of the following is **not** possible?

A Hima warmed up but didn't win the race.

B Hima didn't warm up and still won the race.

C Hima trained well but did not win the 100-m sprint.

D Hima injured herself but still won the 100-m sprint.

31 The members of a book club were asked about the genres they liked to read. The following information was gathered:

- All those who liked fantasy also liked science-fiction.
- All those who liked romance also liked crime.
- None who liked romance also liked science-fiction.

What else must be true?

A None who like fantasy like crime.

B None who like fantasy like romance.

C None who like science-fiction like crime.

D All those who like fantasy also like crime.

32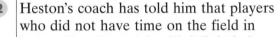
Heston's coach has told him that players who did not have time on the field in last weekend's match will definitely have time on the field in the coming weekend's match.

Heston: 'I had time on the field in last weekend's match so that means I definitely won't get time on the field in the coming weekend's match.'

Which one of the following sentences shows the mistake Heston has made?

A Just because Heston did not have time on the field last weekend, it does not mean he will have time on the field this coming weekend.

B Just because you are in the team does not mean you will be chosen to have time on the field.

C Just because someone who didn't have time on the field last weekend will definitely have time on the field this weekend, it does not mean that anyone who had time on the field last weekend will not have time on the field this weekend.

D Just because Heston had time on the field last weekend, it does not mean he wouldn't like to have time on the field this weekend.

33 Five members of a band check into a hotel after a concert one night and order dinner. The band members are booked into rooms 1, 2, 3, 4 and 5. These rooms are all in a row.

- The drummer ordered pizza and was in the room next to the pianist, who was in room 1.
- The bassist ordered steak.
- The person who ordered soup was in room 3.
- The guitarist was in a room next to the bassist.
- The singer ordered a salad.
- The person who ordered risotto was not in a room next to the guitarist.
- The bassist was in the room next to the singer.

Using the information above, who checked in to room 5?

A the singer

B the bassist

C the guitarist

D the drummer

34 If the sun is out and the temperature is higher than 20 degrees celsius, the washing will dry in less than 4 hours.

Kayla and Taran put their washing out and went inside. They returned outside 4 hours later to find the washing was still damp. They guessed at what the weather might have been.

Kayla: 'The sun was not out.'

Taran: 'The temperature was over 20 degrees celsius.'

If the information in the box is true, which of the following statements is **not** possible?

A Kayla is wrong and Taran is right.

B Both Kayla and Taran are wrong.

C Kayla is right and Taran is wrong.

D Both Kayla and Taran are right.

35 • Miles loves cycling and likes to cycle well.

- If Miles does not cycle well, it's likely because he is tired.
- When Miles doesn't cycle well, he doesn't enjoy it.
- Miles says that once he consistently stops enjoying cycling, he will give it up.
- While he still enjoys cycling, Miles is happy to keep getting up early every morning to do it.

If all the above statements are true, only one of the sentences below **cannot** be true. Which one?

A Miles is often tired but has continued to cycle well.

B Miles isn't tired but has given up cycling.

C Miles had been cycling well but has now given it up.

D Miles has not been cycling well for some time but has not given it up.

36 Kevin, Penny, Toby and Frederick travelled around the city. One went by bus, one went by car, one walked and the other rode a bicycle. One went to Darlington, one went to Maroubra, one went to Mosman and the other travelled to Glebe.

If Kevin went to Darlington, Penny travelled by car, you can't walk to Darlington or Mosman, Toby didn't go to Maroubra and only the bike could make it to Maroubra, which statement must be true?

A Penny travelled to Mosman.

B Penny travelled to Glebe.

C Toby travelled to Mosman.

D Frederick travelled to Glebe.

37 A basketball coach told a group of high-school students the following:
- If you don't train hard, then you won't be selected for my team.
- If you do get selected for my team, then you will play against the best opposition.
- If you don't play against the best opposition, then you won't become an elite player.
- If you aren't an elite player, then you won't get to play for your country.

Patrick, one of the high schoolers, ended up playing basketball for his country.

If all the coach's statements are true, what else must be true?

A He was selected for the team.

B He played against the best opposition.

C He trained hard.

D all of the above

38 Internet scams are big business with people around the world losing billions of dollars each year to scammers. There are many ways a scammer can trick people into giving them money. Some scams advise people they have an overseas inheritance or a lottery win but to collect the money they must firstly pay fees into a foreign bank account. Of course there is no money to inherit or win. Other scams appeal to people's emotions, pleading for money to help someone in need who does not really exist. Some scammers tell you they can prevent your computer from crashing but you must act urgently and give them your passwords. Losses due to internet scams are on the increase globally.

Which statement best expresses the main idea of the text?

A There are many ways a scammer can trick people into giving them money.

B People around the world lose billions of dollars to scammers each year.

C Internet scams are big business with people around the world losing billions of dollars to scammers.

D Losses due to internet scams are on the increase globally.

39 The world's best zoos ensure their animals do not suffer from zoochosis. Captive animals can develop zoochosis, a mental condition where animals in captivity lose their minds through boredom, loneliness, lack of freedom or depression—or because they are abused by their captors. Animals with zoochosis display repetitive, abnormal behaviour, such as rocking, swaying, pacing or self-harm. Antidepressant medication can dull their anxiety but has other harmful side effects such as gastrointestinal upset, weight changes and irregular heartbeats so prevention is better than cure.

Which one of these statements, if true, most **weakens** the above argument?

A The best zoos give their animals antidepressant medication so they don't feel anxious.

B The best zoos house their animals in enclosures that are as close as possible to their habitats in the wild.

C The best zoos offer enrichment activities so animals don't suffer from boredom.

D The best zoos provide adequate medical care and appropriate food.

40 Looking at a car yard from left to right there is a Mercedes, Bentley, BMW, Toyota and Holden. Every day the owner moves the cars around to emphasise different cars to passing customers. On the first day she swaps the Mercedes with the Holden and the Toyota with the Bentley. On the second day she swaps the Bentley with the BMW and the Holden with the Toyota. On the third day she swaps the Bentley with the Holden and the Toyota with the Mercedes. Which cars are now back in their original position?

A the Bentley and the Holden

B the Mercedes only

C the Mercedes and the Bentley

D the Holden and the Mercedes

1 Look at the three-dimensional solid below:

Which is **not** a possible view of the solid?

A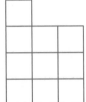

B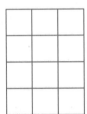

C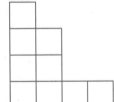

D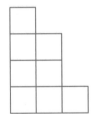

2 Lola's mother has written to the local council. She has suggested that, to protect the local Little Penguin population, dogs should be banned from the walkway around the Point where the colony of penguins have their nesting sites, as there is a high risk of a dog disturbing the nests.

Which one of the following statements, if true, most **strengthens** Lola's mother's argument?

A Dogs, cats and foxes are a threat to Little Penguins.

B When dogs do not get enough exercise, they get overexcited.

C The presence of a dog near a burrow can make Little Penguins abandon their nests.

D People jogging along the walkway have complained about dogs tripping them up.

3 A 3-by-3 cube had a 1-by-1 hole drilled all the way through the centre of it, as shown by the before and after images below:

Before:

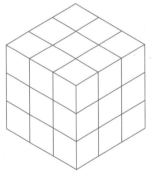

After:

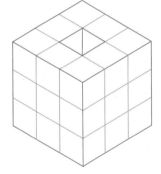

The surface area of a solid is the sum of the area of all of the faces.

What has happened to the volume and surface area of the original solid?

A Both the volume and surface area have decreased.

B The volume has decreased and the surface area has increased.

C The volume has increased and the surface area has decreased.

D Both the volume and surface area have increased.

4 Bilal is designing his own tile. He creates the tile on the right:

If he duplicates this tile, which of the following images can Bilal create?

A  **B**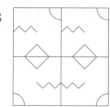

C 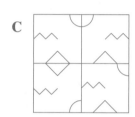 **D**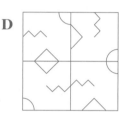

5 World Ranger Day is celebrated every year on 31 July. You might think of rangers as the men or women collecting entrance fees to national parks or leading visitors on park tours but rangers do much more than that. The world's natural heritage is vulnerable to threats like poaching, human–wildlife conflict and wildlife trafficking—and brave park rangers are the front line of defence. They face life-threatening dangers in their daily work apprehending poachers and smugglers or performing search-and-rescue missions. Around the world, over one thousand rangers have died in the line of duty.

Which statement best expresses the main idea of the text?

A Rangers apprehend poachers and smugglers.

B Rangers risk their lives to protect our world's vulnerable animals and natural areas.

C Team Lioness is one of Kenya's first all-women wildlife ranger units.

D National parks are good places to see wildlife in their natural habitat.

For questions 6 and 7, read the information below.

Four classmates are competing for the top prize in Visual Arts at their school. The prize is awarded to the student who scores the highest combined mark from the top three of their four assessment tasks throughout the year.

For example, if Paris scored 9, 2, 8 and 6 in her four tasks, her combined mark for the prize would be 9 + 8 + 6 = 23 as the score of 2 would be discounted.

Each assessment is marked out of 10. The results after Assessment Task 3 stand as follows:

	task 1	*task 2*	*task 3*	*task 4*
Nick	5	8	6	
Kiara	2	8	5	
Mia	10	7	5	
Seth	6	3	6	

6 After Task 4, the students all had equal combined marks from their top three tasks. What did Kiara score in Assessment Task 4?
A 7 **B** 8 **C** 9 **D** 10

7 Instead of handing out four awards, the prize was awarded to the student with the highest fourth-best score. If only one prize was awarded, who won it?
A Nick **B** Kiara **C** Mia **D** Seth

8 The principal at Arlo's school tells the assembly: 'Whoever broke the window must have brought a ball to school and must have been in the playground before school.'

If this is true, which one of these sentences must also be true?

A If Arlo did not break the window, he must not have brought a ball to school.

B If Arlo did not break the window, he must not have been in the playground before school.

C If Arlo brought a ball and was in the playground before school, he must have broken the window.

D If Arlo did not bring a ball to school, he cannot have broken the window.

9 Ruby is in the garden mowing the lawn when her friend Blake arrives.

Blake: 'You love mowing the lawn!'

Ruby: 'No, I don't! It's way too hot!'

Blake: 'So why are you doing it?'

Ruby: 'It's Dad's birthday … and I forgot to get him a present.'

Which one of the following sentences shows the mistake Blake has made?

A Ruby loves mowing the lawn.

B Everyone who mows the lawn loves mowing the lawn.

C Ruby's dad loves mowing the lawn.

D Everyone knows mowing the lawn is hot work.

10 Taylor works at a newspaper. In the office there are clocks on the wall set to the time zones of major cities. Those on the left are ahead of those on the right. Some construction work in the building has shaken the city names—Sao Paulo, London, Sydney, Perth and Toronto—off the wall. Only the clocks are left on the wall:

Taylor knows the following:

• Sydney is 2 hours ahead of Perth.

• Toronto is 5 hours behind London.

If it is 9 am on Tuesday in Sydney, what time is it in Sao Paulo?

A 7 am   **B** 7 pm   **C** 8 am   **D** 8 pm

11 For this question, shapes that are reflections or rotations of each other are considered the same shape. For example:

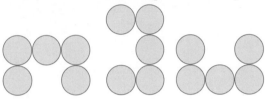

are the same shape.

The following shape can be transformed into three other shapes by moving only one of the small circles to another position:

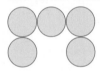

For which shape is this **not** possible?

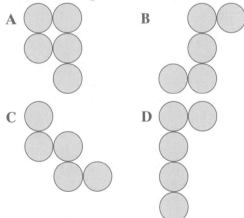

12 Three different shapes are shown below:

Which one of the following arrangements **cannot** be made by putting these three shapes together?

A

B

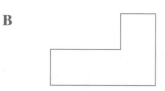

C

D

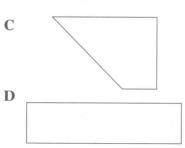

13 A TV station is selecting contestants for a new cooking show. As well as considering each applicant's cooking skills, the show auditioned them and set them a challenge. If an applicant had at least some cooking skills, they only needed to pass the audition. If they had no cooking skills, they needed to have an excellent audition and also do well in the challenge.

David is an experienced cook but was not chosen to be a contestant on the show. What must have been the reason?

A He did badly in the challenge.

B He did not have an excellent audition.

C He failed the audition.

D He did badly in the audition and the challenge.

14 The local hamburger restaurant has a special offer. The deal includes one burger with salad, plus one drink. Customers can also choose to upgrade the deal to include either cheese, an extra patty or a side of chips.

Carlos: 'I'd like the upgrade deal please. I'll have the burger with salad and cheese, a bottle of water and a side of chips.'

Which one of the following sentences shows the mistake Carlos has made?

A Carlos ordered more than the upgrade deal offered.

B Carlos should have ordered a drink or a side of chips, not both.

C The deal is only available on Wednesdays.

D Carlos does not have enough money to pay for the upgrade deal.

15 Faisal said: 'We should try not to use products that contain palm oil. Mass palm-oil plantations are harming the environment and wildlife. I saw on the news that rainforests in Indonesia are being cleared to make way for these plantations. They use fire to clear the land because it is cheap and fast but the fires cause suffocating air pollution and contribute to global warming. Then they replace the rainforests with palm oil plantations—so it also kills the biodiversity that was in the rainforest ecosystem.'

Which one of these statements, if true, most **strengthens** Faisal's argument?

A Palm-oil plantations cause habitat loss for endangered species, such as the orangutan.

B Demand for cheap palm oil continues to grow.

C Palm oil is used to manufacture soaps, cosmetics, processed food and many other items we use every day.

D Palm oil is delivered from the fruit of the palm-oil tree.

16 A circle, a square, a triangle and an ellipse (oval) are used to make a pattern. Each step is made up of the four shapes (shaded in one of four different colours: black, white, grey or blue) placed on top of one another, so in some steps some or all of certain shapes cannot be seen. At each step the order in which the shapes are placed depends on their colour.

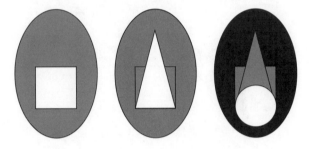

At the fourth step, only a white ellipse can be seen.

What shape will be found immediately beneath the white ellipse?

A a blue triangle

B a grey circle

C a black square

D a black circle

17 Nina said: 'My uncle wants to climb Mount Everest. He's climbed a few other mountains and has been training on the weekends. Dad says it is way too risky and he shouldn't go. But my uncle says Dad is worrying for nothing because there is no risk since he will have a Sherpa guide who knows the way, who will also carry oxygen bottles for the altitude and who will rescue him if he gets in trouble.'

Which one of these statements, if true, most **weakens** Nina's uncle's argument?

A New technology, such as weather prediction systems, helicopters and GPS devices, make climbers feel safer.

B In the last year, a record number of permits were issued to climb the mountain.

C Mount Everest is higher than Nina's uncle has ever climbed before.

D Mount Everest has freezing temperatures, extreme altitude, unpredictable icefalls and avalanches.

18

> To be a successful actor, you need a good memory to remember lines and direction, teamwork skills to work with cast and crew, and creativity to develop characters.

Aida: 'I'm creative and love inventing characters in drama club. I also find it easy to recite poetry from memory. Plus I'm really good at working in a team. I'll definitely be a successful actor.'

Mo: 'I have a really good memory and I prefer to work in a team rather than work alone. But I might not be very creative. So maybe I won't be a successful actor.'

If the information in the box is true, whose reasoning is correct?

A Aida

B Mo

C Both Aida and Mo

D Neither Aida nor Mo

19 There are four teams in the Broken Hill AFL competition.

If each team plays each other five times, and there is a single semifinal and then a grand final, how many games are played throughout the season?

A 17 **B** 30 **C** 32 **D** 62

20 Balloons kill wildlife. If they are released, they can travel hundreds of kilometres before deflating and falling into oceans and waterways. There they are mistaken for food by marine animals and birds. The balloons wrap around other items in the animal's stomach and cause blockages which lead to dehydration, starvation and death. Balloons with strings pose another threat. Wildlife can become entangled in the strings and die.

Which statement best expresses the main idea of the text?

A Balloons fall into oceans and waterways.

B Colourful balloons with strings do not pose any threat to wildlife.

C Balloons are a threat to wildlife.

D Popped balloons look like jellyfish to turtles.

21 If Gia stays up late playing computer games, she's likely to sleep in. If she sleeps in, she won't get to the tryouts on time. If she does get to the tryouts on time, she might be offered a place on the team. Otherwise she doesn't stand a chance.

Based on the above information, which one of the following **cannot** be true?

A Gia stayed up late but was offered a place on the team.

B Gia went to bed early but did not get a place on the team.

C Gia got to the tryouts on time but was not offered a place on the team.

D Gia slept in but was offered a place on the team.

22 A single number is picked from 1 to 9 and added to both the numerator and the denominator of a fraction which is less than one.

What could you say about the new fraction?

A The new fraction is closer to one.

B The new fraction is smaller than the old fraction.

C The new fraction is equal to the old fraction.

D The new fraction is greater than one.

23 Dogs with longer snouts are generally better at scent detection than those with shorter faces.

Marina: 'My dog has a longer face than your dog so my dog must be better at scent detection than yours.'

Eric: 'My dog has a flat face. He mustn't be able to smell anything!'

If the information in the box is true, whose reasoning is correct?

A Marina

B Eric

C Both Marina and Eric

D Neither Marina nor Eric

24 What is the fewest number of coins needed to make $14.50 if you must use at least one of every possible type ($2, $1, 50c, 20c, 10c and 5c)?

A 11 **B** 12 **C** 13 **D** 14

25 To help aid his design, a skate-park designer surveyed a class group to find out how a new skate park would be used. He asked each student to only pick the activity they would most use it for.

He created this graph:

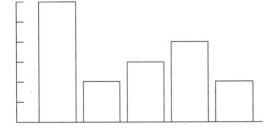

He forgot to label the columns or the axes but he remembered some things about the answers the class gave him.

- More students chose bike riding than rollerblading.
- Twice the number of people chose skateboarding than scootering.
- The number of people who said they would not use the park at all was the same as the number of people who chose rollerblading.

If six people chose skateboarding, how many chose bike riding?

A 6 **B** 4 **C** 3 **D** 2

26

> When Ella arrives home from school, she notices her neighbour has put out his bins.

Ella: 'It must be bin night. I'll remind mum that we need to put ours out.'

Which one of the following sentences shows the mistake Ella has made?

A People only put out their bins on bin night.

B Ella's mum hates putting out the bins.

C People only put out their bins when they're full.

D Ella's neighbour's bins must be full.

27 Marissa is placing five photo frames on the mantelpiece. Each photo frame is a different size. As she is undecided as to how to arrange them, she asks each of her four children to stipulate a rule to help her place them.

They gave the following stipulations:

Child 1: The third-largest frame must be placed furthest to the right.

Child 2: The largest and smallest frames must be next to each other.

Child 3: The largest and second-largest frames must not be next to each other.

Child 4: The largest frame must be to the right of the smallest frame.

While this still gave Marissa some options on how to arrange them, one thing is certain.

Which must **not** be in the centre of the mantelpiece?

A the largest frame

B the second-largest frame

C the second-smallest frame

D the smallest frame

28 Television viewers of the Olympic Games were surveyed to find which of three sports they preferred to view. All those who enjoyed watching canoeing enjoyed watching rowing. Some viewers enjoyed watching archery only and some viewers enjoyed watching all three sports.

Elliot took part in the survey.

Based on the above information, which statement below must be true?

A If Elliot likes two sports only, he must like archery.

B If Elliot likes one sport only, he must like rowing.

C If Elliot likes two sports only, he must like rowing.

D If Elliot likes rowing and archery, he doesn't like canoeing.

29 Three friends were talking about which activity they were going to do on Sunday. They can only choose one activity.

Connor: 'If it rains, then we will play a board game together.'

Grace: 'If it doesn't rain, we are not going to watch a film.'

Jett: 'If the temperature is 25 degrees or over, we will all go to the pool.'

The friends ended up playing a board game together on Sunday.

If the friends were true to their word, what else must be true?

A The temperature was 25 degrees or over.

B The temperature was under 25 degrees.

C It rained.

D It didn't rain.

30 To be successful as a musician, you must be talented and lucky.

If the statement above is true, what must also be true?

A If Layla is not a successful musician, she must not be talented or lucky.

B If Layla is talented and lucky, she must be a successful musician.

C If Layla is lucky, she cannot also be talented.

D If Layla is not talented, she cannot be a successful musician.

31 Five dogs were entered into a competition where they had to run around a racecourse as fast as they could, before being marked for their good behaviour out of a possible score of 5.

- Fido scored higher in behaviour than Rusty.
- Beethoven scored higher than Pongo in behaviour and finished the race behind Fido.
- Doug scored 3 in behaviour and finished the race just behind Rusty.

- Pongo was faster than Fido but not as fast as Doug.
- The dogs that came third and fourth in the race scored equally for behaviour.

If all of the above statements are true, which of the following sentences **cannot** be true?

A Doug scored higher than Rusty for behaviour.

B Rusty scored lower than Pongo for behaviour.

C The dog that won the race scored the same in behaviour as the dog that came fifth.

D The dog that scored second highest for behaviour came second in the race.

32 Ali said, 'Whales are endangered yet every day they struggle to survive against the threats of ship strikes, entanglement in fishing gear and ocean noise.' Tim replied, 'We must save them before it's too late.'

Which one of these statements, if true, most **strengthens** Tim's argument?

A Whales communicate with complex and mysterious sounds.

B Around 360 North Atlantic right whales are left in the world.

C Whales play an important role in the overall health of the marine environment.

D Conservation groups are working to design fishing gear that does not kill whales.

SAMPLE TEST 3

33 Five towns are spread around an area.

- Allansville is halfway between Brighton and Carlisle.
- Dareton is halfway between Brighton and Edgerton.
- Brighton is due east of Carlisle.
- Carlisle is north-west of Edgerton.
- Edgerton is due south of Brighton.

In what direction is Dareton from Allansville?

A south-east   B south-west

C north-east   D north-west

34 Six people are seated at a rectangular table. There is one person at either end and two on each side of the table. These are the arrangements:

- John is diagonally opposite Percy.
- Kamal is opposite Angela.
- Jim is between Kamal and Percy, and diagonally opposite Nick.

Who is seated between John and Angela?

A Nick   B Kamal   C Jim   D Percy

35 The student council at Ying's school wanted to start some clubs. They did a survey of all students at the school and found the following:

- Everyone who would like a film club would also like a drama club.
- Everyone who would like a drama club would also like a comedy club.
- No-one who would like a drama club would like a coding club.

Which one of these sentences can be concluded from the above information?

A If Ying would like a film club, she would not like a coding club.

B If Ying would not like a coding club, she would not like a comedy club.

C If Ying would not like a film club, she would not like a comedy club.

D If Ying would like a comedy club, she would also like a drama club.

36 One person each from England, France, Germany and Italy were asked which languages they spoke fluently. Each person speaks the language of their own country fluently and speaks no languages other than those mentioned here.

- Markus speaks German, French and English.
- Laura speaks Italian and German.
- Paulo speaks English and French.
- Jan speaks Italian and English

Which of the following statements is **not** definitely true?

A If Markus is from France, then Jan is from Italy.

B If Paulo is from England, then Laura is from Germany.

C If Markus is from Germany, then Paulo is from France.

D If Paulo is from France, then Jan is from Italy.

37

> If it is raining, there must be clouds in the sky.

Andy: 'There are clouds in the sky so it must be raining.'

Ben: 'It isn't raining so there must not be clouds in the sky.'

If the information in the box is true, whose reasoning is correct?

A Andy only

B Ben only

C Both Andy and Ben

D Neither Andy nor Ben

38 Levi's swimming coach told him that any swimmers who did not get a chance to compete last month will definitely be selected to compete this month.

Levi: 'Oh no, I competed last month. That means I won't be selected to compete this month. Maybe I can be a timekeeper.'

Which one of the following sentences shows the mistake Levi has made?

A Just because someone did not compete last month, it does not mean they would not have liked to compete.

B Just because someone who did not compete last month will be selected this month, it does not mean someone who competed last month will not be selected this month.

C Just because someone is selected to compete, it does not mean they will compete.

D Levi's coach did not mention who would be timekeeping.

39 Whenever Alice's little brother Finn accidentally leaves his toy elephant at day care, he always cries on the way home.

Alice: 'Thankfully Finn didn't leave his elephant at day care today so he won't cry on the way home.'

Fran: 'I saw Finn crying yesterday when you were going home. He must have left his elephant at day care yesterday.'

If the information in the box is true, whose reasoning is correct?

A Alice

B Fran

C Both Alice and Fran

D Neither Alice nor Fran

40 A hair-regrowth company claimed: 'Nine out of 10 men who used our product kept or regrew their hair.'

What is the most logical conclusion that can be drawn from this statement?

A The product might work for some users.

B The product definitely works for some users.

C The product stops hair loss for up to 90% of users.

D The product promotes hair regrowth in 90% of users.

1 A cuckoo bird on a cuckoo clock springs out of its doors twice for every strike of the bell. The bell on the clock strikes the number of the hours every hour. For example, at 8 o'clock the clock strikes eight times and at 9 o'clock it strikes nine times.

How many times does the cuckoo bird spring through its doors each day?

A 156 **B** 312 **C** 600 **D** 1200

2 **Evie:** 'Dad made a chocolate sponge cake last night. It was for my birthday dinner.'

Joe: 'Yum! Chocolate sponge cake is my favourite. It must be yours too!'

Evie: 'No, I don't like sponge cake. I prefer ice-cream cake. But Dad wanted to try a new recipe.'

Which one of the following sentences shows the mistake Joe has made?

A Evie's dad doesn't know how to make ice-cream cake.

B Chocolate sponge cake is easier to make than ice-cream cake.

C Everyone gets their favourite cake on their birthday.

D Chocolate sponge is Evie's favourite cake.

3 Three siblings—Angus, Bethany and Callan—all scored in their games of soccer at the weekend. Their mother asked them how many goals they each scored.

Angus: 'If you multiply our individual totals together, you get 24.'

Bethany: 'The sum of our goals adds to the number of pets we have.'

Callan: 'I scored the most goals but if you add Angus and Bethany's total together, they beat me.'

How many pets does the family have?
A 8 **B** 9 **C** 10 **D** 12

4 I usually catch the bus home from work. I get on at the first stop and have about 10 km to travel so I usually nod off to sleep. I normally fall asleep when the bus has about three times as far to go as it has already travelled. Halfway through the trip I tend to wake up and then I fall asleep again when the bus has three-quarters of the remaining distance to go. I wake up just in time to get off at the right bus stop. For what portion of the trip do I usually sleep?

A I usually sleep for five-eighths of the trip.

B I usually sleep for three-eighths of the trip.

C I usually sleep for one-half of the trip.

D I usually sleep for one-quarter of the trip.

5 • Dora has to to practise piano after school.

• She has an exam next week.

• If she doesn't practise, she'll probably fail.

• If she fails the exam, her parents won't be happy.

• If her parents are happy, they might let her go to Kiyomi's party.

• Otherwise there's no way they'll agree.

If all the above statements are true, only one of the sentences below **cannot** be true. Which one?

A Dora did not practise but her parents said yes to the party.

B Dora practised but her parents did not let her go to the party.

C Dora's parents were unhappy with her but they let her go to the party.

D Dora's parents were happy with her but they did not say yes to the party.

6. Three different shapes are shown below:

Which one of the following arrangements **cannot** be made by putting these three shapes together?

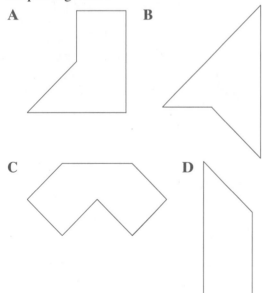

A   **B**

C   **D**

7. After departing Stop A, a bus arrived at Stop B, where three passengers got off and eight got on. At Stop C half the passengers got off and two got on. At Stop D a third of the passengers got off and no-one got on. There are 10 passengers remaining on the bus.

How many passengers were on the bus immediately after it departed Stop A?

A 21   **B** 31   **C** 41   **D** 51

8. It is feasible to refill an electric vehicle's battery for free. You can refill an EV battery wherever there is a power point. As power points are just about everywhere you just need to find the ones that are free. Some shopping centres, restaurants, hotels or tourist attractions offer no-cost EV charging. Even some workplaces let you fill up the battery while you work. Of course if you have solar power at home, you can also refill for free there. And don't forget, electric cars generate their own free fuel while driving. If you slow down earlier and back off the accelerator when going down hills, the electric motor will reverse and feed electricity back into the battery pack. That's fuel for free!

Which statement best expresses the main idea of the text?

A Electric cars can generate their own fuel.

B It is hard to find a power point to refill an EV.

C Some local councils have public EV-charging stations.

D Free fuel is possible with electric vehicles.

9. The school principal was trying to decide who to invite to speak to students at the careers open day. She decided to let all the students have a secret vote. This is what she found:

• Wildlife carer was more popular than football player.

• Police officer was less popular than firefighter, which was two spots behind author and three spots behind wildlife carer.

• Author was more popular than football player but less popular than wildlife carer.

Which one of these sentences can be concluded from the above information?

A Firefighter was more popular than football player.

B Police officer was the least popular choice.

C Author was less popular than firefighter.

D Football player tied with author.

10 Jun has some tiles left over from his bathroom renovations. He decides he'd like to tile a pattern around the base of his birdbath by repeating a four-tiled square design:

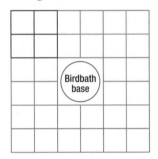

He has the following tiles left:

10 ×   15 ×   25 ×

Which of the following designs is Jun **not** able to use?

A 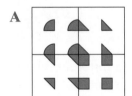   B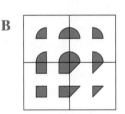

C 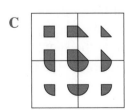   D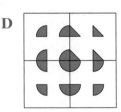

11 Jack's parents won't allow him to use social media. They worry that social media requires too much personal information and is dangerous for children. They also say that social media is too distracting for children and worry that Jack would get sidetracked and not be able to focus on homework and other school activities.

Which one of these statements, if true, most **weakens** Jack's parents' argument?

A Children need boundaries, both online and offline.

B Other children, as well as pets, already have social-media accounts.

C Social media makes bullying easier and can also lead to identity theft.

D Children taught to use social media in a healthy way will become more responsible users in the future.

12 Samim has four hens in his chook pen. Each morning, he collects three white eggs and one brown egg. Samim can divide his chook pen in half using a partition. He plans to separate the hens over a number of nights to find out which hen is laying the brown egg. He can only use the two sections of the chook pen and he cannot stay up all night watching the hens.

If he knows that every hen is laying one egg, what is the minimum number of nights Samim needs to guarantee he will know which hen is laying the brown egg?

A 1   **B** 2   **C** 3   **D** 4

13 A 3-by-3 cube had an edge altered, as shown by the before and after images below:

Before:

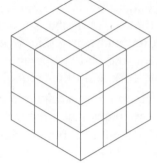

After:

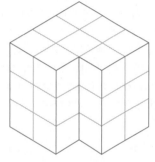

The surface area of a solid is the sum of the area of all of the faces.

What has happened to the volume and surface area of the original solid?

A The volume has increased and the surface area has decreased.

B The volume has decreased and the surface area has increased.

C Both the volume and surface area have decreased.

D Both the volume and surface area have increased.

14 The local community theatre was offering free tickets for their opening night. Members on their mailing list had to apply online for up to four tickets by giving their membership number. If someone on the mailing list was not a member, they had to apply in person at the box office and at the same time sign up to be a member. Anyone who was not a member and not on the mailing list was not eligible for the free tickets.

Mr Lin is a member of the theatre and is on the mailing list. He wanted three tickets but he did not get them. What must have been the reason?

A He did not apply online.

B He ordered too many tickets.

C He forgot to take his membership card to the box office.

D The box office was closed.

15 Mr Smith set his class a challenge to read a greater variety of books. Students had to keep a separate record of how many fiction books and how many nonfiction books they read. At the end of the challenge, students added their tallies for fiction and nonfiction together to get the overall number of books read. Mr Smith awarded prizes for most fiction read, most nonfiction read, most read overall and greatest variety read. Yitong and Ben tied for the prize for most read overall.

Yitong: 'If we read a different number of fiction books, then we must have read a different number of nonfiction books too.'

Ben: 'And if we read the same number of nonfiction books, then the number of fiction books we read must be the same too.'

Based on the information in the box, whose reasoning is correct?

A Yitong

B Ben

C Both Yitong and Ben

D Neither Yitong nor Ben

16 The houses in a particular street are numbered sequentially up one side of the street to the end, continuing back along the other side of the street ending opposite house number 1. Each house is the same size and is directly opposite a house on the other side of the street.

Lincoln lives in number 16 and his good friend Amy lives directly across the street in number 133. Rishabh lives in house number 100 and his friend Miles lives directly across the street from him.

What is Miles's house number?

A 47   **B** 48   **C** 49   **D** 50

17 Today, 'birdbrain' means a person who is a bit silly or scatterbrained. But the truth is, birds have brains more complex than any known animals except mammals. Research on a newly discovered bird fossil suggests that it was the brains of some dinosaur birds that played a part in their survival when all other known dinosaurs died out in the mass extinction. The parts of the brain where speech, thought and emotion occur in humans are larger in living birds than in the dinosaurs that died out. This suggests these functions could be connected to the ancestors of living birds surviving the mass extinction. Of course, mammal and bird brains evolved very differently but never has 'birdbrain' been such a compliment!

Which one of these statements, if true, most **strengthens** the above argument?

A Greater intelligence and living in more complex social groups may have helped dinosaur birds survive.

B Birds have been found to make tools and understand abstract concepts.

C Bird skeletons are brittle and rarely survive in the fossil record.

D Some birds can recognise paintings by Monet and Picasso.

18 Mr Robertson said that students who worked in the school garden but did not have a chance to help in the garden kitchen last term will definitely get a chance to help in the garden kitchen this term.'

Anya: 'Oh, I really wanted to help in the kitchen this term. But I worked in the garden and helped in the kitchen last term, so that means I'll miss out on the kitchen this term.'

Which one of the following sentences shows the mistake Anya has made?

A Just because someone did not help in the kitchen last term, it does not mean they would not have liked to.

B Just because the school had a garden kitchen last term, it does not mean it will have one this term.

C Just because someone is given a chance to help in the garden kitchen, it does not mean they will want to help in the garden kitchen.

D Just because someone who did not get a chance to help in the garden kitchen last term will get a chance to this term, it does not mean someone who helped last term will not get a chance this term.

19 Lift passes for a ski resort were priced as follows:

daily	3-day	weekly (7 consecutive days)
$60	$140	$250

I plan to go skiing in August on the following dates:

4, 5, 6, 9, 10, 11, 12, 14, 17, 18.

How much is the cheapest combination of tickets I can purchase?

A $500 **B** $510 **C** $520 **D** $530

20 In a survey of school students, everyone who was interested in karate was also interested in lacrosse. Everyone interested in lacrosse was interested in hockey, but no-one who was interested in lacrosse was interested in fencing.

Based on the above information, which one of the following must be true?

A If Jade is not interested in fencing, she is not interested in hockey.

B If Jade is interested in karate, she is not interested in fencing.

C If Jade is not interested in karate, she is not interested in hockey.

D If Jade is interested in hockey, she is also interested in lacrosse.

21 Bree said: 'We just found out that everyone in my class has to give a speech next week. My topic is going to be climate change.'

Max: 'You must know a lot about climate change!'

Which one of the following sentences shows the mistake Max has made?

A Students learn a lot about a topic when they prepare a speech.

B Students only give speeches about topics they know a lot about.

C Max's teacher assigned the topic of the speech.

D Max is an experienced speaker.

22 Throughout the Edinburgh Festival, Daisy is performing her one-woman show twice a day on Monday, Wednesday and Friday, and three times a day on Saturday and Sunday.

If the festival runs for 21 days exactly, how many times will she perform?

A 15 **B** 18 **C** 30 **D** 36

23 Katy said: 'In a battle between a great white shark and a saltwater crocodile, the crocodile would win.' Cameron disagreed: 'No, the great white shark would win for sure. For a start it is heavier than the crocodile and wider than the crocodile's mouth. It's also twice as fast. Plus the crocodile will need to surface to breathe which will give the shark a chance to attack from beneath.'

Which one of the following, if true, most **strengthens** Cameron's argument?

A Saltwater crocodiles need to fit their target in their mouth to cause maximum damage.

B Saltwater crocodiles have a stronger bite force than great white sharks.

C The teeth of great white sharks are replaceable and could fall out during a struggle.

D A shark is more likely to die from its injuries than a crocodile.

24 A census was taken of 120 horses in a paddock to determine their colour pattern. The results were as follows:

black	21
bay	46
dappled grey	14
chestnut	39

When the information was put into a sector graph, one of the pattern types was missed out.

This is the sector graph that was created:

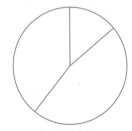

Which pattern was missed out?
A black
B bay
C dappled grey
D chestnut

25 When viewed from above, an object looks like the picture shown below:

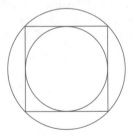

Which of the following is **not** a possible view from the side?

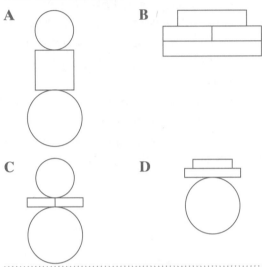

A
B
C
D

26 Na's teacher said the class could watch a movie to celebrate the end of term. He said he would choose a movie from whichever genre students preferred. He asked students to rank three preferred genres from a list of five potential genres. To tally the results, he awarded a genre three points each time it was a student's first choice, two points each time it was a student's second choice and one point each time it was a student's third choice. He found that:

• All his students preferred comedy to fantasy.

• Adventure was more preferred than science-fiction.

• Musicals were more preferred than adventure or science-fiction.

• Fantasy was preferred over adventure.

Based on the above information, which one of the following sentences **cannot** be true?

A The most preferred genre was comedy.

B Science-fiction was the least preferred genre.

C Fantasy was more preferred than science-fiction.

D Musicals could not have been the most preferred genre.

27 While James was reading on his verandah, five vehicles passed his house: one truck, two white cars, a red car and a green car.

- The truck did not pass first or fifth.
- The red car came directly after a white car.
- There were two vehicles between the green car and the second white car.

If the first car is white, which must be true about the fourth vehicle?

A It is white.

B It is red.

C It is green.

D It is a truck.

28 A group of people completed a survey on which ice-cream flavours they liked. The information below was deduced from the results:

- Some people who like strawberry also like chocolate.
- All those who like vanilla also like both chocolate and strawberry.
- All those who like pistachio like strawberry but nothing else.
- More students like pistachio than like only chocolate.

What else must be true?

A More students like chocolate than strawberry.

B Some students like strawberry only.

C More students like vanilla than pistachio.

D Strawberry is the most popular flavour.

29 Three bushwalkers were making deals about the day ahead:

Oscar: 'If we manage to walk over 10 km today, I'll set up all of our tents.'

Petra: 'If Oscar sets up all our tents, I'll build the fire.'

Camelia: 'If Oscar doesn't set up the tents tonight, I will not cook dinner for everyone.'

If the bushwalkers stuck to their deals and Camelia cooked dinner for everyone, what else must be true?

A They walked over 10 km and Petra built the fire.

B Oscar set up all the tents and Petra built the fire.

C They walked over 10 km and Oscar set up all the tents.

D They walked less than 10 km and Petra did not build the fire.

30 Winnie was told by her piano teacher that if she practised her scales and her performance piece every day, she would definitely pass her third-grade piano exam.

Winnie didn't pass her third-grade piano exam.

If the piano teacher's information above is correct, which of the following **cannot** be true?

A Winnie practised her scales every day.

B Winnie practised her performance piece every day.

C Winnie practised her scales and performance piece every day.

D Winnie didn't do any practice.

31 The Jones, Sullivan, Khan, Edgecombe, Muscat and Brady families all want to book into a holiday house over a four-week period. Each family wants to spend two weeks at the house but the house is only big enough to accommodate three families at a time.

- The Jones family don't wish to holiday with the Sullivans.
- The Khan family wants to spend a week with the Joneses and a week with the Sullivans.
- The Edgecombe family wants to spend at least a week with the Khan family.
- Every family except the Muscat family want to holiday for two consecutive weeks.

If the Jones family book in for the first two weeks and every family's wishes are met, which family definitely won't get to holiday with the Brady family?

A the Edgecombe family

B the Sulllivan family

C the Jones family

D the Muscat family

32 Indigenous rangers care for country. They manage fire through controlled burning, reduce feral animal impacts, control invasive weeds, maintain cultural sites and care for our most endangered animals. Every day, they actively promote the ideals of Indigenous culture. This work benefits every Australian across our massive continent.

Which statement best expresses the main idea of the text?

A Australia has a problem with feral animals.

B Australia is a massive continent with multiple environmental pressures.

C Indigenous rangers do important work caring for country.

D Indigenous rangers work in biosecurity compliance.

33 Of three barrels of fruit, one contains apples only, another contains oranges only and the third is a mix of the two. The barrels are labelled APPLE, ORANGE and MIXED. A mistake leads to the labels being switched around so that none of the barrels are labelled correctly.

By only picking one piece of fruit out at a time, and without looking into the barrels, what is the maximum number of picks you must make in order to relabel the barrels correctly?

A 0   B 1   C 2   D 3

34 The Reyes family have a rooster in the backyard. Its crowing is very loud and will always wake them. If the rooster crows, it only does so after sunrise.

Mr and Mrs Reyes are lying in bed with the curtains drawn.

Mr Reyes: 'I haven't heard the rooster; it must be before sunrise.'

Mrs Reyes: 'No, I'm sure it's later than that. We must have slept through the crowing.'

Whose reasoning is correct?

A Mr Reyes only

B Mrs Reyes only

C Both Mr and Mrs Reyes

D Neither Mr nor Mrs Reyes

35

Whenever the yellow light on the heater flashes on and off it means the filter needs to be cleaned.

Kinta: 'Oh no! The yellow light is on continuously. The filter must be completely blocked!'

Ava: 'No, the light has to flash. It isn't flashing now so that must mean the filter is fine.'

If the information in the box is true, whose reasoning is correct?

A Kinta

B Ava

C Both Kinta and Ava

D Neither Kinta nor Ava

36 Beyond Brisbane is a talent program that identifies and trains young athletes in Olympic sports. As well as considering age and motor skills, the selectors for the program run a standing jump test and an agility test.

If your motor skills are excellent for your age, you only have to pass the standing jump test.

If you do extremely well in the agility test and well in the standing jump test, your motor skills are not important.

Karel's motor skills are excellent for his age but he was not selected for the program. What must have been the reason?

A He did not pass the agility test.

B He did not do well in the standing jump test.

C He did not pass the standing jump test.

D He did not do extremely well in the agility test.

37 Four teams—GWS, Essendon, West Coast and Fremantle—are all hoping to finish in the top eight of the AFL ladder after the last game of the regular season. There are two spots up for grabs. Before the last round, the following statements are true:

• For GWS to make the top eight, they need to win or two of the other three teams need to lose.

• For Essendon to make the top eight, they need to win or they could lose, as long as West Coast and Fremantle both lose.

• For West Coast to make the top eight, they need to win and two of the other three teams need to lose. Or they must win and at least one of GWS and Essendon must lose.

• For Fremantle to make the top eight, they need to win and two of the other three teams need to lose.

• None of the four teams play each other in the last round.

GWS and Essendon finished the season inside the top eight. Which of the following **cannot** be true?

A GWS and Essendon both lost.

B West Coast and Fremantle both won.

C GWS lost and West Coast won.

D Fremantle lost and Essendon won.

38 A marine biologist said: 'Australian humpback dolphins off the coast are being handfed illegally, with harmful consequences. Handfeeding can decrease calf survival rates, cause aggression within pods or towards humans and increase the number of boat-related dolphin injuries. Studies show handfeeding dolphins can even lead to mothers not teaching their young vital life skills, putting the entire pod and population at risk.'

Which one of these statements, if true, most **strengthens** the marine biologist's argument?

A A public awareness campaign is underway to inform tourists about the consequences of handfeeding dolphins.

B The whole ecosystem in the area is fragile and unnatural feeding of dolphins negatively impacts all the diverse marine life.

C People can be fined up to $10 000 for handfeeding the dolphins.

D Hundreds of thousands of tourists visit the area every year.

39 Sophie's mother loves gardening. This year she entered a tomato in the 10th annual biggest tomato contest at the local community fair. In the contest, gardeners are allowed to enter only one tomato. Ribbons are then awarded for first, second and third biggest tomato. This year there is also a special ribbon to anyone who has entered the contest every year for its ten-year history.

Sophie: 'There are only two gardeners who have entered the contest every year for its ten-year history. So that means five gardeners will get ribbons.'

Which one of the following sentences shows the mistake Sophie has made?

A The gardeners who had entered every year might have come first, second or third.

B We don't know how many gardeners entered the contest.

C One gardener might have been awarded a ribbon for more than one tomato.

D Some gardeners might deserve a prize if they missed only one year of the contest.

40 If a saltwater crocodile egg is incubated at 31.7 degrees Celsius, it will be a male. Anything above or below this temperature will most likely produce a female.

Colin and Rishi saw the above information on a sign at a crocodile sanctuary. They then made some observations about the saltwater crocodiles they could see:

Colin: 'That crocodile could have been incubated at 31.7 degrees Celsius.'

Rishi: 'That crocodile could have been incubated at a temperature above 31.7 degrees Celsius.'

If the information in the box, as well as the friends' comments, are true, what combination of crocodiles are the two friends definitely **not** looking at?

A two female crocodiles

B two male crocodiles

C one male and one female

D They are looking at the same crocodile.

1 Solve this problem:

$$2 \times 8 + 9 + 7 \times 6 = ?$$

67	144	192	15	246
A	B	C	D	E

2 A car travels at 40 km per hour. How far will it travel in three and a half hours?

A 160 km
B 100 km
C 140 km
D 120 km
E 150 km

3 What is three and a quarter hours before 9.30 pm in 24-hour time?

1815	0645	1830	0615	1805
A	B	C	D	E

4 Rose flips a coin two times. What are the chances of getting a head then another head?

A one chance in eight
B one chance in six
C one chance in four
D one chance in two
E one chance in three

5 Chocolates cost $8 for a kilogram. How much would 250 g cost?

A $4.00
B $2.00
C $2.50
D $3.00
E $1.80

6 What distance does a car travel if its average speed is 80 km per hour and it travels for three and a half hours and then slows down to 70 km per hour for two hours?

A 420 km
B 400 km
C 380 km
D 460 km
E 410 km

7 A shop sells sweets for either 50 cents or 10 cents. A customer spent $8 and took home a total of 24 sweets. How many 50-cent sweets did he or she buy?

10	12	16	14	18
A	B	C	D	E

8 What is the area of the shaded part?

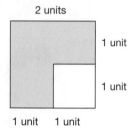

A 2 square units
B 5 square units
C 4 square units
D 3 square units
E 2.5 square units

9 A plane travels at 800 km per hour and a fast train travels at a quarter of this speed. How much time will it take the train to travel 400 km?

A $\frac{1}{2}$ hour

B $\frac{3}{4}$ hour

C 1 hour

D $1\frac{1}{2}$ hours

E 2 hours

10 Three trucks are equal in weight to two trucks and two sedans. What fraction of the weight of a truck is the weight of a sedan?

A one-quarter
B one-half
C one-third
D three-quarters
E two-thirds

11 The opposite faces of a dice add up to seven. If the top faces of four dice show one, two, three and four, then what is the total of the four opposite sides?

20	17	19	18	21
A	B	C	D	E

12 Bruce multiplied the largest three-digit even number by the smallest two-digit number that is a multiple of 3. Which of these is his result?

A 1198   B 9990
C 11988   D 11976
E 11999

13 The area of the circle is 480 cm². What is the shaded area?

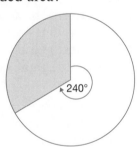

A 120 cm²   B 140 cm²
C 160 cm²   D 150 cm²
E 180 cm²

14 A number has a remainder of 3 when divided by 4 and a remainder of 5 when divided by 6. What is the smallest possible number greater than 40?

25	59	43	51	47
A	B	C	D	E

15 The shape consists of 20 identical squares. Corinne shades $\frac{3}{5}$ of the shape.

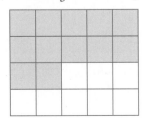

How many more squares must be shaded to leave $\frac{1}{5}$ of the squares **not** shaded?

2	3	4	5	6
A	B	C	D	E

16 Today is 16/8/21 and it is Pablo's birthday. Last year his age was a multiple of 6. In 2 years, Pablo's age will be a multiple of 5. If he was born last century, which of these could be Pablo's age today?

13	23	43	44	53
A	B	C	D	E

17 How many lines of symmetry can be drawn on this shape?

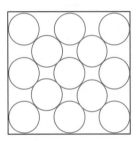

3	4	1	0	2
A	B	C	D	E

18 The net below forms a cube on which opposite faces multiply to the same number.

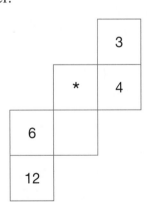

What is the number represented by ⋆?

6	8	1	10	2
A	B	C	D	E

19 Molly made a pattern of balls. The order was a blue, two yellows, a green, three reds and then a purple, and then she repeated the pattern many times. What colour is the 36th ball?

A red

B blue

C green

D yellow

E purple

20 In a magic square, numbers in each row, column and diagonal add to the same number. What is the number that is represented by the *?

	5		16
*			11
12	10	9	15
7		18	

19	17	4	8	6
A	B	C	D	E

21 Here are the first six numbers in a sequence.

1, 4, 9, 16, 25, 36 …

Evie picks two numbers in the sequence. The difference is 19. What is the sum of the numbers?

141	221	251	161	181
A	B	C	D	E

22 A circle is drawn on a whiteboard. Indiana shades $\frac{1}{3}$ of the shape, Sienna shades $\frac{1}{4}$ and Ava shades $\frac{1}{5}$. What fraction of the original shape has **not** been shaded?

$\frac{11}{60}$	$\frac{1}{4}$	$\frac{1}{60}$	$\frac{1}{6}$	$\frac{13}{60}$
A	B	C	D	E

23 Nicola has a box of 40 apples. She eats 10% of the apples and gives half of the remaining apples away. If she uses four apples to make an apple pie, how many apples remain?

11	14	16	18	20
A	B	C	D	E

24 Laine wrote this number sentence.

$$80 \div \boxed{?} - (2 + 6) \times 4 = 8$$

What is the missing number?

1	2	4	8	10
A	B	C	D	E

25 Ronan is making a pattern out of white and blue tiles. Here is the line of tiles he has already arranged. He wants the pattern to have two lines of symmetry. What is the smallest number of tiles he needs to place on the right side of his pattern?

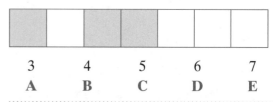

3	4	5	6	7
A	B	C	D	E

26 The diagram shows two triangles. An equilateral triangle has a side length of 4 cm. An isosceles triangle has a perimeter twice as long as the equilateral triangle. If one side is 3 cm longer than another side, which of these is a possible side length of the isosceles triangle?

Not to scale

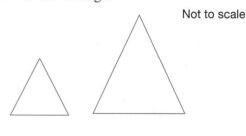

5 cm	11 cm	8 cm	9 cm	12 cm
A	B	C	D	E

27 Which number sentence describes the statement 'Twice the sum of four and the product of two and six is greater than the difference between eighteen and the quotient of eight and four'.

A $2 \times 4 + 2 \times 6 > 18 - 8 \div 4$

B $2(4 + 2 \times 6) > (18 - 8) \div 4$

C $2 \times (4 + 6) > 18 - 8 \div 4$

D $2 \times (4 \times 2 + 6) > 18 - 8 \div 4$

E $2(4 + 2 \times 6) > 18 - 8 \div 4$

28 Here is a pattern of towers made from small cubes each with a volume of 8 cm³.

The pattern continues. What is the height of the tower with a volume of 168 cm³?

10 cm	12 cm	14 cm	16 cm	20 cm
A	B	C	D	E

29 A container, originally full of water, is leaking. When it is one-quarter empty it holds 84 L. What amount of water is in the container when it is one-quarter full?

28 L	30 L	36 L	42 L	252 L
A	B	C	D	E

30 A plane leaves New York at 2220 on Tuesday to fly to Dubai. The plane arrives in Dubai at 1905 on Wednesday. If Dubai if 8 hours ahead of New York, how long was the flight?

A 12 hours 45 minutes

B 11 hours 45 minutes

C 13 hours 45 minutes

D 11 hours 15 minutes

E 12 hours 15 minutes

31 The length of rectangle I is half the length of rectangle II which is a quarter the length of rectangle III. All three rectangles have the same width.

How many rectangle Is would be needed to cover rectangle III?

12	2	8	4	16
A	B	C	D	E

32 A group of students were asked what their favourite colour was.

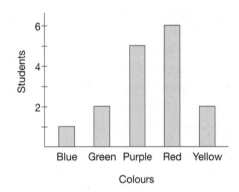

Here are three statements Jackson made about the graph.

1. Four more students liked purple than yellow.

2. A quarter of the students liked green or yellow.

3. Twice as many students liked red than the total of the students who liked blue or green.

Which of Jackson's statements is/are correct?

A statements 2 and 3 only

B statement 1 only

C statement 2 only

D statement 3 only

E statements 1, 2 and 3

33 The letter N has been drawn. Which of these transformations will result in an image identical to the original N?

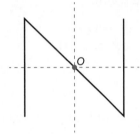

A a rotation of 90º in a clockwise direction around *O*

B a reflection about the vertical line

C a reflection about the horizontal line

D a rotation of 90° in an anticlockwise direction about *O*

E a rotation of 180° around *O*

34 Two identical squares overlap to form a shape. What is the area of the new shape?

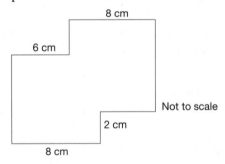

80 cm²   84 cm²   92 cm²   96 cm²   116 cm²
  A   B   C   D   E

35 Students recorded the colour of 60 cars in the teachers' car park. The results are shown in the sector graph below.

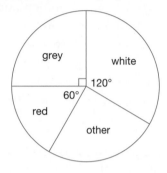

Here are three statements made about the graph.

1. There were 15 grey cars.

2. Half the cars were white or red.

3. There were 12 cars that were not white, red or grey.

Which of these statements is/are correct?

A statement 1 only

B statements 2 and 3 only

C statements 1 and 2 only

D statement 2 only

E statements 1, 2 and 3

40 MIN

1 Which of these is another way of expressing the square root of 169?

A $5 \times 12 - 6 \times 7 \div 2$
B $3 \times (5 \times 2) \div (16 \div 2)$
C $(13 \times 2) - 21 \div 7 - (14 \div 2)$
D $(13 \times 10) \div (5 \times 2)$
E $13 \times 10 + 13 \times 2 + 1$

2 What would a quarter of a kilogram of fetta cheese, 300 grams of parmesan and 400 grams of cheddar cost?

FETTA CHEESE: $19.80/kg
CHEDDAR: $13.70/kg
HAM: $18.40/kg
SALAMI: $12.80/kg
OLIVES: $10.80/kg
PARMESAN: $22.40/kg

A $18.20
B $17.15
C $19.65
D $16.85
E $17.40

3 In which sums are the answers even numbers?

I 234×367 II $365 + 424$

III $433 - 321$ IV 987×329

V $968\,472 \div 12$

A I, III and IV
B I, II and V
C I, III and V
D III, IV and V
E II, III and V

4 Anthony counts backwards from 120 by twelves and John counts backwards from 120 by tens. Excluding 120 and zero, how many of the same numbers do they say?

2	0	6	3	1
A	B	C	D	E

5 Here is a figure.

Which one of these drawings could make the shape above?

6 A system using these three symbols ☺☺☹ is used for numbers from 1 to 40. For instance, some samples of the numbers are given below.

☹ = 1   ☹☺ = 4   ☹☺ = 9
☹☹ = 2   ☺ = 5   ☺ = 10
☹☹☹ = 3   ☺☹ = 6   ☺☹ = 11

How should 27 be written using this same code?

A ☺☺☺☹☹
B ☹☺☹☹☹☺
C ☺☹☺☹☺
D ☺☺☹☹☹☹☹☹☹☹
E ☺☺☹☹☹☹☹

7 A sales assistant makes sales of $100 on the first day. Every day the sales increase by 10%. On the second day the sales are $110 and on the third day $121. How much is made on the fifth day?

A $133.10   B $139.44   C $146.41
D $158.85   E $177.16

8 Find the missing number in the square marked *. (Hint: This is not a magic square. Consider the numbers in adjacent squares in each row and column.)

10		2
	18	
	32	*

36	28	6	14	36
A	B	C	D	E

9 Which of the following numbers is the greatest common factor of 64 and 16?

4	8	12	1024	32
A	B	C	D	E

10 What is the missing number in this series?

144   169   ?   225

196	198	192	194	200
A	B	C	D	E

11 The assets of a large company are around fifty million dollars when rounded to the nearest million. Which one of the following could be the exact figure in the annual account?

A $5 260 000   B $5 600 000
C $49 507 861   D $44 909 999
E $55 000 999

12 If (8 ✳ 2) × (9 ❖ 3) = 72, what do the symbols ✳ and ❖ represent?

A ✳ equals minus and ❖ equals plus
B ✳ equals times and ❖ equals minus
C ✳ equals minus and ❖ equals times
D ✳ equals plus and ❖ equals minus
E ✳ equals times and ❖ equals plus

13 A worker earns $10 per hour. After seven hours the worker is paid $15 per hour. There is also one hour unpaid break midway through the shift.

How much would this worker earn if he/she worked a shift from 6 am until 5 pm?

$130	$125	$110	$115	$120
A	B	C	D	E

14 What is the area of the unshaded portion of the shape below?

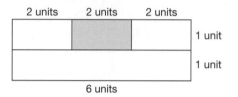

A 12 square units
B 10 square units
C 14 square units
D 8 square units
E 9 square units

15 A box containing 10 jars of seafood sauce weighs 2600 g. How much would six jars of the same kind weigh?

A 1.80 kg
B 1.3 kg
C 1.56 kg
D 1.72 kg
E 1.66 kg

16 Steve and Sue downloaded a movie and started watching it at 8:50. Sue watched the whole movie which finished at 10:30. Steve watched the movie until he went to bed at 10:00. What percentage of the movie had Steve watched?

70%	55%	60%	75%	65%
A	B	C	D	E

17 A ball is dropped from a height of 50 m. After it hits the ground, it always bounces to a height of $\frac{2}{5}$ its previous height.

Through what distance has the ball travelled by the time it hits the ground a third time?

106 m	88 m	84 m	53 m	94 m
A	B	C	D	E

18 The monthly maximum temperatures of a town are graphed below.

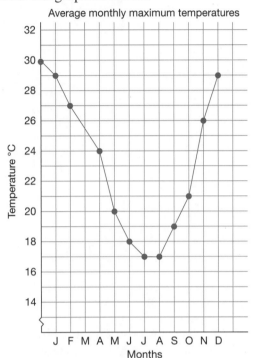

Average monthly maximum temperatures

Here are three statements made about the graph.
1. The average monthly maximum temperature for August was 24°.
2. The difference between the highest and lowest temperatures was 13°.
3. The biggest rise in temperature in a month was 5°.

Which of these statements is/are correct?

A statements 1 and 2 only
B statement 2 only
C statement 3 only
D statements 2 and 3 only
E statements 1, 2 and 3

19 Brooke used coloured tiles to make a pattern. The tiles were blue, green and red.

B	G	R	R	B	G	R	G

Brooke wants to add more tiles to the right of the existing tiles so that the pattern has a vertical line of symmetry.

What is the smallest number of tiles Brooke needs to add?

2	3	4	5	7
A	B	C	D	E

20 Leigh used matches to make this sequence of patterns.

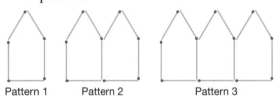

Pattern 1   Pattern 2   Pattern 3

How many matchsticks would be used to make the shape in Pattern 20?

40	17	88	80	81
A	B	C	D	E

21 The diagram shows a large square split into rectangles and squares. The four small squares are identical in size. What is the area of the shaded rectangle?

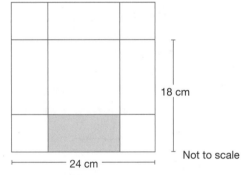

18 cm

24 cm   Not to scale

A 108 cm²
B 112 cm²
C 72 cm²
D 84 cm²
E 64 cm²

22 Sharni has a set of glasses each with a capacity of 240 mL. She pours all the juice from a 2-litre container into the glasses.

She decides to fill the glasses to only $\frac{5}{6}$ of their total capacity to prevent spillage. How many glasses will she use?

5	10	12	4	8
A	B	C	D	E

23 A bag contains green, blue and red balls. The probability of choosing a red ball at random is $\frac{2}{5}$, and the chance of choosing a blue ball is $\frac{1}{4}$. What is the smallest possible number of green balls in the bag?

4	6	7	8	9
A	B	C	D	E

24 Pete took 2 hours to drive from Wagga Wagga to West Wyalong. His average speed for the trip was 75 km/h. How much less time would the trip have taken if he increased the average speed by 25 km/h?

A 10 minutes   B 20 minutes
C 60 minutes   D 45 minutes
E 30 minutes

25 The number line shows the location of X, which is in the middle of 4.38 and 5.1.

4.38 X 5.1

What decimal is represented by X?

4.62	4.69	4.79	4.73	4.74
A	B	C	D	E

26 If it takes 1 hour 35 minutes to paint $\frac{1}{3}$ of a wall, how much more time will it take to finish the job?

A 2 hours 45 minutes
B 2 hours 35 minutes
C 2 hours 50 minutes
D 3 hours 10 minutes
E 2 hours 55 minutes

27 Alyson flew from Paris to Los Angeles leaving at 0840 Friday. The flight took 11 hours 50 minutes. What time did Alyson arrive if Paris is 9 hours ahead of Los Angeles?

A 2330 Friday
B 0630 Saturday
C 1130 Friday
D 1330 Friday
E 1130 Saturday

28 The shape has been formed using identical rectangles arranged to form a square. What is the area of each rectangle?

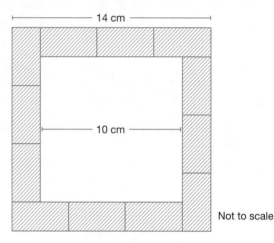

Not to scale

6 cm^2	8 cm^2	10 cm^2	12 cm^2	16 cm^2
A	B	C	D	E

29 The diagram shows a logo. How many lines of symmetry can be drawn on the logo?

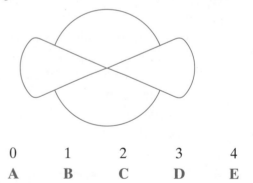

0	1	2	3	4
A	B	C	D	E

30 At a party, Dakota faces north and is blindfolded. She is spun 270° in a clockwise direction, then 225° in an anticlockwise direction. The blindfold is now removed. What direction is Dakota facing?

A north-east
B east
C south-east
D south-west
E north-west

31 Frida thinks of a number. She multiplies her number by 6 and then divides this result by 3. She adds 4 and then subtracts 2. She subtracts the first number she thought of. She then adds 5. She again subtracts the original number she thought of. What is her answer?

9	6	1	4	7
A	**B**	**C**	**D**	**E**

32 The mass of a mango and tomato is 600 g. The mass of the tomato and an apple is 540 g. The mass of the mango and the apple is 620 g. What is the total mass of the three pieces of fruit?

A 780 g
B 880 g
C 960 g
D 980 g
E 1760 g

33 A school raised money for a Winter Appeal for the Homeless. The amounts raised by different year groups are listed in the graph below.

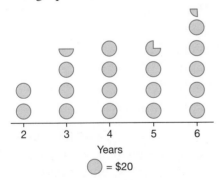

Years

◯ = $20

What was the total amount raised by the school?

$345	$360	$365	$370	$400
A	**B**	**C**	**D**	**E**

34 What is the obtuse angle between the hands of an analog clock at half past nine?

95°	100°	99°	101°	105°
A	**B**	**C**	**D**	**E**

35 A box contains 12 coloured balls. The balls are either red (R), blue (B), green (G), yellow (Y) or purple (P).

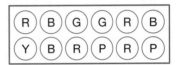

A ball is chosen at random from the box. Here are three statements.

1. The probability of choosing a red ball is $\frac{1}{4}$.
2. A green ball is twice as likely to be chosen as a yellow ball.
3. The probability of choosing a yellow or purple ball is the same as choosing a blue ball.

Which of these statements is/are correct?

A statement 1 only
B statements 2 and 3 only
C statement 3 only
D statements 1 and 2 only
E statements 1, 2 and 3

1 In 2 years' time I shall be three times as old as my youngest son. In 10 years' time, the sum of our ages will be 80. How old do you think my son is now?
A 8 years old
B 12 years old
C 14 years old
D 16 years old
E 18 years old

2 The battery on a watch is beginning to fail and the watch is losing time. It is losing about six minutes for every hour it moves. The watch was correctly set at 9 am. What would be the time shown on the watch when the correct time is now 3.30 pm?
A 2.51
B 4.09
C 2.24
D 3.03
E 3.09

3 What is the smallest four-digit number in which the digit in the tens place is half the digit in the hundreds place?
A 1010
B 1201
C 1420
D 1120
E 1210

4 What is the missing number marked * in this magic square of numbers from 1 to 16, so that the lines down, lines across and diagonals all add up to the same total?

*	3	2	13
5	10		8
9	6	7	
4		14	1

11	12	15	16	10
A	B	C	D	E

5 Three hobbyists had a total of 27 budgerigars. The first had three more than the third. The second had three times the number of the first. How many budgerigars did the third collector have?

5	2	1	3	6
A	B	C	D	E

6 What is the total of two hundred thousand dollars and two hundred thousand cents?
A $220 000
B $202 000
C $200 200
D $202 200
E $200 020

7 A foolish gambler placed one dollar on the first square of a chess board on the first day, then two dollars on the next square on the second day, then four dollars on the third square on the third day and eight dollars on the fourth square on the fourth day and so on, hoping to be able to double it on each of the 64 squares. On what day would he need more than $10 000 to be placed on a square?
A on the 15th day
B on the 11th day
C on the 13th day
D on the 14th day
E on the 12th day

8 A cricketer averages 45 for 10 innings. How many runs must be scored in the 11th innings to raise the average to 50?

50	60	90	100	75
A	B	C	D	E

9 Even numbers starting at two were added together. Their total equals 306. How many numbers were added together?

34	153	17	27	37
A	B	C	D	E

10 Which of these statements is true?

A The product of an odd number and an even number is an odd number.

B The sum of two odd numbers is an even number.

C The product of two odd numbers is an even number.

D The sum of an even number and an odd number is an even number.

E The product of two even numbers is an odd number.

11 Each week 10 per cent of my salary goes towards savings. This leaves me with $180. How much do I earn?

A $200   B $189   C $198

D $209   E $190

12 4   7   16   43   124   ?

What is the next number in this series?

367	372	243	289	357
A	B	C	D	E

13 A whole number is multiplied by four. What must the answer be?

A The answer must be a squared number.

B The answer must be a prime number.

C The answer must be divisible by eight.

D The answer must be an even number.

E The answer must be a factor of 64.

14 I usually catch the bus home from work. I get on at the first stop and have about 10 km to travel so I usually nod off to sleep. I normally fall asleep when the bus has about three times as far to go as it has already travelled. Halfway through the trip I tend to wake up and then I finally fall asleep again when the bus has three-quarters of the remaining distance to go. I wake up just in time to get off at the right bus stop. For what portion of the trip do I usually sleep?

$\frac{5}{8}$	$\frac{3}{8}$	$\frac{1}{2}$	$\frac{1}{4}$	$\frac{1}{3}$
A	B	C	D	E

15 Use the numbers 1, 2, 3, 4, 5, 6 and 7 to make fractions smaller than one. How many different fractions smaller than one can be made using two of these numbers?

42	21	33	17	28
A	B	C	D	E

16 The letters XYZ stand for different numbers. What is the value of X in the following multiplication?

$$\begin{array}{r} XYZ \\ \times \quad 3 \\ \hline ZZZ \end{array}$$

2	1	5	8	0
A	B	C	D	E

17 In some exams you lose marks for incorrect answers. A student answered 30 questions in a test and was given a score of 20 on the test. The student scored one mark for each correct answer and lost one mark for each incorrect answer. How many questions were answered correctly?

20	27	25	23	24
A	B	C	D	E

18 Water flow to a chemical process is increased under pressure by double its volume every minute. The process takes 2 hours to reach maximum flow. What is the time at which the flow is at half its maximum rate?

A after 1 hour

B after 1 hour 57 minutes

C after 1 hour 30 minutes

D after 1 hour 59 minutes

E after 59 minutes

19 The rectangle contains two identical shaded squares. What fraction of the rectangle is **not** shaded?

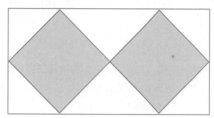

Not to scale

$\frac{1}{4}$	$\frac{3}{4}$	$\frac{1}{3}$	$\frac{1}{2}$	$\frac{2}{3}$
A	B	C	D	E

20 The smallest angle in a triangle is one-quarter the size of the largest angle. If the sum of these two angles is 115°, which of these is the size of the largest angle in the triangle?

65°	96°	25°	94°	92°
A	B	C	D	E

21 The odometer in Dante's car shows 79811. He drives for 2 hours 30 minutes at an average speed of 84 km/h. What is the odometer reading at the end of his trip?

A 79961
B 80011
C 80021
D 80031
E 80041

22 Two adults and three children go to the movies. An adult ticket costs $22 and a child ticket is half price. Each person has an ice cream which costs $5. Which of these is the number sentence used to find the total cost, in dollars?

A $5[22 \times 2 + (22 \times 3) \div 2]$
B $22 + 5 \times 2 + (22 \times 3) \div 2 + 5$
C $22 \times 2 + (22 \times 3) \div 2 + 5 \times 5$
D $(22 + 5) \times 2 + (22 \times 3) \div 2 + 5$
E $(22 + 5) \times 2 + (22 \times 3) \div (2 + 5)$

23 Levi drew a pattern of rectangles.

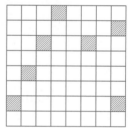

Levi continues the pattern. One of his rectangles has a perimeter of 78 cm. What is the area of that rectangle?

A 410 cm²
B 380 cm²
C 400 cm²
D 440 cm²
E 420 cm²

24 What is the smallest number of squares that need to be shaded if the diagram is to have one line of symmetry?

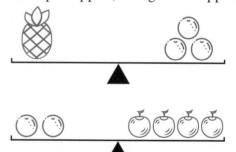

2	3	4	5	6
A	B	C	D	E

25 Jack uses pan balances to compare the mass of pineapples, oranges and apples.

How many apples have the same mass as two pineapples?

12	8	9	6	15
A	B	C	D	E

26 In a bag there are coloured balls. The probability of randomly selecting a green ball is 0.2, and the probability of a red ball is 0.5. The rest of the balls are purple. If 12 balls in the bag are green, how many are purple?

14	16	18	20	24
A	B	C	D	E

27 Four identical cubes are stacked on top of each other. The total volume of the stack is 32 m³. What is the sum of the area of the faces of each cube?

24 m²	12 m²	48 m²	36 m²	60 m²
A	B	C	D	E

28 A container is filled to three-quarters full. It contains 360 L of water. How much water is in the tank when it is two-thirds full?

300 L	305 L	310 L	320 L	323 L
A	B	C	D	E

29 A container is filled with 20 L of detergent and has a mass of 26 kg. When 5 L of detergent is poured from the container, the mass is now 20 kg. What is the mass of the empty container?

1.5 kg	500 g	1 kg	4 kg	2 kg
A	B	C	D	E

30 The graph shows the coins in Eve's money jar.

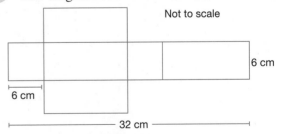

How much money does Eve have in the jar?

$33.50	$28.25	$34.75	$32.50	$31.50
A	B	C	D	E

31 The diagram shows a regular octagon. Two parts of the shape are shaded.

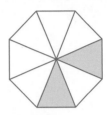

The shape is rotated clockwise into the position shown below.

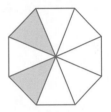

Through what angle has it been rotated?

45°	90°	135°	225°	270°
A	B	C	D	E

32 Four identical squares of side length 2 cm are removed from the corners of a square with side 8 cm. What fraction of the original square remains?

$\frac{1}{4}$	$\frac{2}{3}$	$\frac{9}{16}$	$\frac{5}{8}$	$\frac{3}{4}$
A	B	C	D	E

33 The diagram shows the dimensions of a net.

Not to scale

6 cm

6 cm

32 cm

When the solid is formed, what is the volume?
A 320 cm³
B 360 cm³
C 648 cm³
D 420 cm³
E 192 cm³

34 Here is a spinner with numbers written on eight equal sectors.

There is a number missing. The probability of spinning a factor of 6 is the same as a multiple of 2. What could be the missing number?

1	3	5	8	10
A	B	C	D	E

35 A group of students were surveyed to find the number of televisions in their homes. The graph shows the results of the survey.

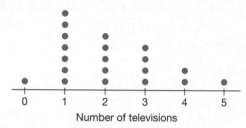

Number of televisions

Here are three statements about the graph.
1. Twenty students were surveyed.
2. There was a total of 42 television sets in the students' homes.
3. 60% of the students had at least two televisions.

Which statement(s) is/are correct?

A statement 2 only
B statement 3 only
C statements 1 and 2 only
D statements 1 and 3 only
E statements 1, 2 and 3

SAMPLE TEST 4

40 MIN

1 One worker can make 24 products in an hour on a job and another worker can make 36 products an hour on the same task. They were both used on the production job. How many minutes would it take them to make 25 products?

25	30	35	40	45
A	B	C	D	E

2 How many more small blocks would be required to complete a large cube that is four by four blocks in size?

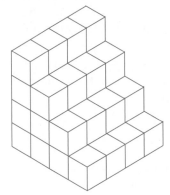

A 40
B 34
C 30
D 24
E 28

3 Find the missing number in the square marked *. There is a pattern across and down. (Hint: you may have to find some of the other numbers before you can find the number you want.)

10	*	18
12	18	
	26	

8	22	30	48	14
A	B	C	D	E

4 Which number below can be divided evenly by eight but when it is divided by 12 there is eight left over?

160	152	120	136	168
A	B	C	D	E

5 Line B is one-quarter the length of line A and line C is one-half the length of line B. What fraction of line A is line C?

$\frac{1}{6}$	$\frac{1}{7}$	$\frac{1}{8}$	$\frac{1}{10}$	$\frac{1}{12}$
A	B	C	D	E

6 A box is 12 cm by 9 cm by 15 cm and we have to fill it with blocks. There are four different types of blocks from which you can choose.

I blocks 3 cm by 3 cm by 3 cm
II blocks 6 cm by 9 cm by 3 cm
III blocks 5 cm by 6 cm by 4 cm
IV blocks 3 cm by 5 cm by 5 cm

Which blocks would you choose to fill the box so that there is as little wasted space as possible?

A I or II only
B III or IV only
C I or III only
D II or IV only
E I only

7 A group of five pupils has an average score of 80 while another group of 10 pupils has an average of 70. Which of these is closest to the average of the 15 pupils altogether?

75	77.3	73.3	71.3	75.3
A	B	C	D	E

8 A box of 15 chocolates weighs 250 g. After you have eaten five chocolates the box weighs 175 g. How many grams does the empty box weigh?

20 g	18 g	17 g	25 g	15 g
A	B	C	D	E

9 By first finding the value of the letters A, B, C and D, what is the value of U?

$$
\begin{array}{r}
U3D \\
\times\ UB \\
\hline
CC7A \\
D68A \\
\hline
B8BA
\end{array}
$$

3	2	5	4	6
A	B	C	D	E

10 This is the arrow on a dynamometer which measures the strength of a person's grip. What approximate reading does the arrow indicate?

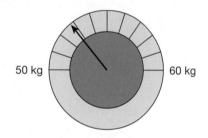

50 kg   60 kg

A 53.2 kg   B 50.3 kg   C 50.29 kg
D 52.9 kg   E 53.5 kg

11 A system using these two symbols ☺☹ is used for numbers. For instance, some samples of the numbers are given below.

☹ = 0   ☺☹☹ = 4
☺ = 1   ☺☹☺ = 5
☺☹ = 2   ☺☹☹☺ = 9

How is 11 written using this same code?

A ☺☺☹☺
B ☹☹☺☹
C ☺☹☹☺☺
D ☺☹☹☹
E ☺☹☹☹☺

12 A stamp collector numbered the rare stamps in a collection. From left to right the one penny kangaroo stamp was number eight. From right to left it was number ten. How many rare stamps were in this collection?

15	16	17	18	19
A	B	C	D	E

13 The length of a rectangle is three centimetres more than three times its width. Its perimeter is 54 cm. What is its width?

A 4 cm
B 6 cm
C 8 cm
D 10 cm
E 9 cm

14 At a meeting, parents and teachers were seated in a row. There were six teachers next to at least one parent and four of them were sitting with parents on either side. There was also a teacher at the end of the row who only had another teacher on one side. How many parents were at this meeting?

5	6	7	8	9
A	B	C	D	E

15 A flight from Adelaide to Sydney takes around two hours. The time difference is half an hour between these two States, with South Australia half an hour behind NSW. If a plane leaves Adelaide for Sydney at 9 am. (South Australian time) when would it arrive in Sydney in Eastern Australian time?

A 12 noon
B 11.30 am
C 11 am
D 10.30 am
E 12:30 pm

16 21 25 39 ? 97

What is the missing number in this series?

43	54	63	75	73
A	B	C	D	E

17 A student revised 81 questions one day. On the next day the student revised two-thirds of those questions. Each day after that the student continued to revise two-thirds of the previous day's work. How many questions did the student revise on the fifth day?

22	20	18	16	24
A	B	C	D	E

18 There is a way to work out the total of a set of counting numbers starting from one without having to add them all up one by one. You simply multiply half the number by the number itself, then add half the number again. What is the total of the first 50 counting numbers (that is, from 1 to 50)?

1250	1275	1300	1325	1350
A	B	C	D	E

19 When you multiply the ages of Anthony and John you get 176. What could be the total of their ages?

27	31	33	36	38
A	B	C	D	E

20 This shape is made from 72 small cubes. How many of the small cubes in this shape have other small cubes above and below as well as to the front and back and also on each side?

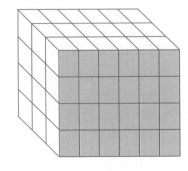

4	6	8	12	16
A	B	C	D	E

21 In a knockout competition, losers do not continue. There are 16 competitors. How many matches will need to be played to find the eventual winner?

16	17	18	19	15
A	B	C	D	E

22 A batch of 30 products on an assembly line are graded in terms of quality as A, B, C, D and Reject. One-half of the products are graded B, one-sixth are graded C, one-fifth are graded D and the numbers of A-rated products and Rejects are equal. How many products are rejected?

2	3	4	5	6
A	B	C	D	E

23 How many of these shapes have more than five lines of symmetry?

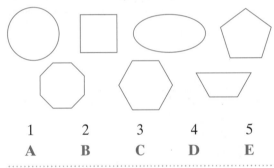

1	2	3	4	5
A	B	C	D	E

24 The sector graph shows the hair colour of 72 students.

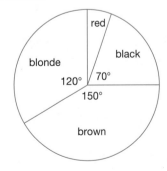

How many students have red or black hair?

20	16	9	10	18
A	B	C	D	E

25 Eleni is playing with her doll collection. When she divides them into groups of 5 there are 3 left over. When she divides them into groups of 6 there are 4 left over. If she has between 30 and 80 dolls, how many are in her collection?

73	58	78	68	53
A	B	C	D	E

26 Nine identical squares each have a perimeter of 40 cm. The squares are joined together to make a larger square. What is the area of the large square?

A 900 cm^2

B 1200 cm^2

C 1600 cm^2

D 2400 cm^2

E 1800 cm^2

27 The shape is to be reflected across the dotted line.

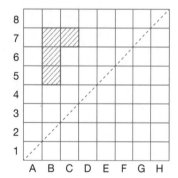

Which of these squares is **not** in the image of the shape?

A E2

B G4

C F2

D G2

E G3

28 Mitchell has a coffee cart business that is operated six days a week. Many of Mitchell's customers use their own cups. The graph shows the number of cups provided by the business each day.

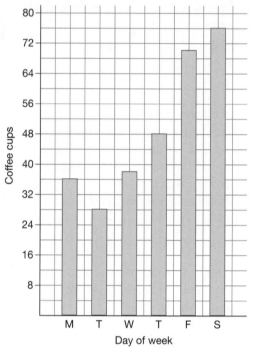

Here are three statements made about the graph.

1. Twice as many cups were used on Saturday as on Wednesday.
2. More than 100 cups were used on Monday, Tuesday and Wednesday.
3. There were 50 fewer cups used on Tuesday and Wednesday than on Thursday and Friday.

Which of these statements is/are correct?

A statement 1 only

B statement 2 only

C statement 3 only

D statements 1 and 2 only

E statements 1, 2 and 3

29 Three friends are counting to 200. Jess starts at 6 and counts by 5s. Verity starts at 7 and counts by 6s. Ash starts at 9 and counts by 8s. Which of these is a number that all girls count?

131	136	126	181	121
A	B	C	D	E

30 What is the value of
[120 − 48 ÷ 4 × 8 − 4] ÷ 20?

7	4	1	1.4	2
A	B	C	D	E

31 Here are some numbers in a pattern.

... 16, 23, 30, 37, 44 ...

If 30 is the fifth number in the pattern, what is the 50th number?

352	340	342	344	345
A	B	C	D	E

32 The arrow is pointing to the letter T. The arrow is moved in a clockwise direction to X. Through how many degrees is the arrow moved?

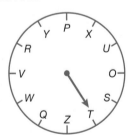

90°	120°	150°	240°	270°
A	B	C	D	E

33 A bag contains 10 cards numbered 1 to 10. One card is removed. Another card is chosen at random. The probability of this number being less than 6 is the same as the probability that it is odd. Which of these could be the number originally removed?

4	9	2	7	8
A	B	C	D	E

34 A square of side 16 cm is split into two equal rectangles. A diagonal is drawn on the square. What is the area of the shaded trapezium?

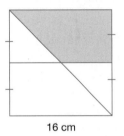

16 cm

60 cm²	64 cm²	72 cm²	80 cm²	96 cm²
A	B	C	D	E

35 The arrows on two spinners are spun and a score is the result of multiplying the two numbers.

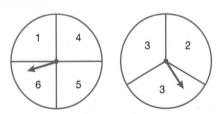

Here are three statements.
1. The highest possible score is 18.
2. The probability of a score of 12 is $\frac{1}{4}$.
3. A score greater than 8 is equally as likely as a score that is an even number.

Which statement(s) is/are correct?

A statement 1 only
B statement 2 only
C statement 3 only
D statements 1, 2 and 3
E statements 2 and 3 only

A **narrative** is a text that tells a story about events in a way that entertains and interests the reader. It can be true or imaginary; funny, thrilling or serious. A narrative should keep the reader interested right to the end. It should encourage the reader to read on.

Your own experiences are extremely useful when writing narratives. A narrative can be written in the first person (that is, it uses the personal pronoun *I*) or in the third person (written about other people).

Your conclusion should be satisfying and suit your story.

Write a narrative containing several paragraphs on **one** of the following topics:

- a snowman
- a scarecrow
- a statue
- a robot
- an alien.

Before you start writing, think about:
- the who and where (orientation) of your story
- the events that take place in your story
- how you will conclude your story.

Remember to:
- quickly plan your story before you start writing
- write in correctly formed sentences and take care with paragraphing
- pay attention to the words you use, your spelling and punctuation
- write neatly but don't waste time
- quickly check your work once you have finished.

On page 131 is an example of an imaginative narrative response to this question, which draws on the personal experiences of the author. Note that this response was not written under test conditions. There is also a marking checklist on page 135.

SAMPLE TEST 2

A **report** relates the particulars of an incident by reconstructing factual information.

A factual newspaper report is an objective (impersonal) recount of a true event, usually by someone not personally involved in the situation. Its purpose is to inform and, at times, entertain.

A report may also recall historical events, such as the lives of interesting people or significant events in society the writer may not have been involved in. Such texts are written from an impersonal point of view, as though the writer is communicating with someone who wants to be informed. These reports are written in the third person using impersonal pronouns such as *he* and *they*.

Choose **one** of the following topics and write a newspaper report containing several paragraphs with a brief conclusion based on an opinion or comment on the topic:

- a newly discovered and interesting historical feature, such as a cave containing Indigenous art
- a sporting event
- efforts to save an endangered species (plant or animal)
- how something has changed (a town, school testing, surfboards)
- a community volunteer project (lifesaving, wildlife rescue, caring for the aged).

Before you start writing, think about:

- where and when the subject of the report occurred
- the events that take place in your report and the issues they raise
- how you (or others) felt or reacted to the subject of the report; you may briefly comment on the events as you write about them.

Note: In a test situation your report can be fictitious.

Remember to:

- plan your report before you start writing
- write in correctly formed sentences
- group relevant information in paragraphs
- pay attention to the words you use, your spelling and punctuation
- write neatly but don't waste time
- quickly check your work once you have finished.

On page 132 is an example of a newspaper report that draws on the personal experiences of the author. Note that this response was not written under test conditions. There is also a marking checklist on page 135.

A **persuasive text** (exposition or opinion) is used to 'argue' the case for or against a particular action, plan or point of view—to *persuade* others to see it your way. A persuasive text needs to be well organised and clear so readers will understand and be convinced by your arguments. A persuasive text responds to an issue or an event. The issue may be contentious or controversial.

The text may include personal opinions and uses the personal pronoun *I*. You will be expected to give your reasons and perhaps also some arguments for those who oppose the idea. This is an opportunity to counter such ideas.

Choose **one** of the following topics and write a persuasive text containing several paragraphs with a conclusion based on an opinion in the text:

- Skateboard riding should be banned on footpaths.
- Tracks for bikes should be provided in parks.
- National parks should be opened for trail bike riding.
- Drones should be restricted to rural areas.
- Beaches are not the place for recreational driving.

Before you start writing, think about:

- the issues involved in your chosen topic
- arguments in favour of your stance; you may add comments as you write about them
- how someone may react to your opinion; an alternate viewpoint (keep it brief)
- finishing with a strong conclusion.

Remember to:

- plan your persuasive text (list your arguments) before you start writing
- write in correctly formed sentences and take care with paragraphing
- pay attention to the words you use, your spelling and punctuation
- write neatly but don't waste time
- quickly check your work once you have finished.

On page 133 is an example of a persuasive text that draws on the personal opinions of the author. Note that this response was not written under test conditions. There is also a marking checklist on page 136.

A **recount** is the retelling of an event. It usually tells the events in the order they happen: the chronological order.

A personal recount is something that involves the writer and uses the personal pronoun *I*. A recount can also recall historical events: the lives of interesting people or significant events in society the writer may not have been involved in. Such texts are written from an impersonal point of view. These recounts are written in the third person using impersonal pronouns such as *he* and *they*.

Choose **one** of the following topics and write a personal recount containing several paragraphs with a brief conclusion based on an opinion or comment on the topic:

- a visit to an unusual store (antiques, bears, hobbies)
- a special museum visit (military, vintage machines, mining)
- a factory producing food or drink (chocolate, pies, juice)
- a visit to a place that practises old trades or skills (blacksmith, glass blowing, jewellery).

Before you start writing, think about:

- where and when the recount takes place
- the events that take place in your recount and the issues they raise
- how you (or others) felt about the event; you may comment on the events as you write about them.

Remember to:

- plan your recount before you start writing
- write in correctly formed sentences and take care with paragraphing
- pay attention to the words you use, your spelling and punctuation
- write neatly but don't waste time
- quickly check your work once you have finished.

On page 134 is an example of a persuasive text that draws on the personal opinions of the author. Note that this response was not written under test conditions. There is also a marking checklist on page 136.

READING Test 1 Page 1

1 A 2 B 3 D 4 D 5 C 6 A 7 C 8 B 9 C
10 C 11 A 12 C 13 B 14 A 15 F 16 B
17 G 18 A 19 E 20 D 21 C 22 B 23 A
24 D 25 B 26 C 27 B 28 A 29 D 30 A

1   It is mere chance that Ariadne catches sight of Theseus and feels pity for him. If she hadn't given him the ball of yarn, he would be unlikely to have escaped from the Labyrinth. B is incorrect because, although catching sight of the Gorgon plays a significant part, it is a scene that is set up deliberately. Since A is the correct answer and B is incorrect, neither C nor D can be correct.

2   Theseus is hailed as a hero and Perseus earns his place among the heroes. A is incorrect because Theseus kills a minotaur not a man. C and D are incorrect because Ariadne acts bravely but not heroically and Athené is a female god and not technically a woman.

3   Theseus chose to take on the minotaur to defend his family's honour when he had no real obligation to do so. His unselfishness led to his saving his people from years of suffering and loss. A, B and C are incorrect because his actions are not particularly characterised by common sense, obedience or intelligence.

4   Ariadne offers lifesaving advice to Theseus about using the ball of yarn to find his way out of the Labyrinth. Athené's advice to Perseus about the Gorgon saves many lives. A is incorrect because, although Ariadne is a princess, Athené is a goddess. B is incorrect because only Athené is close to the Immortals. C is incorrect because we are not told what either of the women look like.

5   The minotaur is part man and part bull while the Gorgon, a maiden, is given snakes for hair and an eagle's claws for hands. This implies that A, B and D cannot be correct.

6   Minos was confident of victory because he knew no-one could find their way from the Labyrinth so that even if they managed to kill the minotaur, they could not escape. B is incorrect because Minos could not count on the obedience of the Athenians. C is incorrect because, although the minotaur made victory likely, it was the Labyrinth that ensured success. D is incorrect because his daughter's loyalty could not be relied upon.

7   Perseus's words suggest something horrifying may be about to happen. The tension is high as we know what the fate will be for anyone who obeys his command. A and B are incorrect because his words do not offer release from anxiety or any kind of humour. D is incorrect because there is nothing disappointing about this moment; it is the high point of the drama.

8   Polydectes and his guests are so frightened they turn pale and are unable to move. They are literally petrified (*petra* means stone in Greek), or turned to stone, when they look at the Gorgon's head. A, C and D are incorrect because the transformation is instant and other emotions, such as being scared, frightened or worried, do not fully describe their condition accurately.

9   The narrator is referring to the girl who is sitting on her front steps looking towards her. A is incorrect because the narrator refers to herself as 'Me' at this stage of the poem. B is incorrect because the girl's mother is no longer alive. D is incorrect because the narrator's mother does not appear until later in the poem.

10 It was at the beach that the girls had the best of times together. They 'whirl' through the air, 'slice' through the water and sing together acting as though they are a family. A, B and C are incorrect as those occasions are described in less positive ways.

11 There is a hint of disapproval and discomfort in the word 'used', as though the narrator feels the girl is borrowing something that doesn't belong to her. It is not as clear or

powerful a feeling as anger or sadness but there is no hint of pleasure in it either. This makes B, C and D incorrect.

12 The narrator is envious of the girl still having some ice cream left to eat when she has finished hers. A, B and D are incorrect as there is no evidence that the narrator feels any of these strong emotions.

13 We are told the girl has lost her mother. This creates sympathy for her but is slightly undercut by her being unaware of how intrusive she can be at times. Further, her behaviour with the ice cream does seem deliberate and rather mean. A, C and D are incorrect because they assume the attitude towards her is consistent throughout the poem.

14 The question mark raises questions about the nature of the relationship between the girls. Can it be a real friendship when so many ambiguous feelings are involved? B and C are incorrect because strong feelings of anxiety or despair are not involved. D is incorrect because a question mark raises questions rather than adds confidence.

15 In the previous sentence the author is talking about how long elephants spend eating and drinking. This sentence gives details of what an elephant eats: It consumes large quantities of grasses, leaves, bamboo, bark, roots and other vegetation. The sentence that follows gives details of the amounts of water an elephant drinks.

16 In the previous sentence the author is talking about the composition of an elephant herd. This sentence identifies the leader of these herds: These are led by the oldest female, the matriarch. The sentence that follows explains how matriarchs use their memories to guide the herds that depend on them.

17 In the previous sentence the author states that an elephant's trunk has many functions. This sentence lists some of its functions: It uses it to breathe (its nostrils run the length of its trunk), feed, smell and bring water to its mouth and spray it over its body. The sentence that follows explains how it achieves another of its functions.

18 In the previous sentence the author is talking about elephant's tusks. This sentence adds the information that the ivory part of their tusks is sought after: The visible part of the tusk, the ivory, has always been in high demand. The sentence that follows explains that poaching of elephants to get this ivory has led to numerous elephant deaths.

19 In the previous sentence the author is talking about the 1989 ban on trading of ivory. This sentence describes some of the effects of this ban: This had some protective effects, as did the Chinese and American Presidents enacting ivory bans in their own countries. The sentence that follows explains that in more recent times the ban has lost much of its effectiveness and is part of the reason some species are endangered.

20 In the previous sentence the author is talking about how the recent increase in poaching has led to the endangerment of some species of elephants. This sentence adds the information that some species have suffered more than endangerment: Some species of elephant are now extinct. The sentence that follows gives information about the three species that currently survive.

Note: The unused sentence is C.

21 The author expresses her disapproval and distress at the unjust nature of the punishment. A, B and D are incorrect because they do not include complaints about injustice.

22 You can work out the words of the author's great-great grandfather quoted in his diary were written in 1915. A and D are incorrect because they don't include any quotations. C is incorrect because the quoted words were written in 1793, which is in the 18th century.

23 The author reports discovering that her relatives signed a petition that was completed by women and helped women win the vote. B and C are incorrect because, although they explore personal connections to history, they are not made because of a gender-related matter. D is incorrect because there is no personal connection made.

24 The author uses words such as 'alluvial', 'nuggets', 'drifts', 'lodes' and 'quartz matrix' in explaining the kind of gold first found at the diggings in Australia. A, B and C are incorrect because they only include infrequent technical terms.

25 The author does not fully explain what happened to her great-great grandfather during or after the war. We can work out he survived and had a child but we aren't told the full story. A, C and D are incorrect because we are told the outcome of the events in these texts.

26 John's one-word answer, 'Dead', is distressing because learning of a troubled child with no parents nor any memory of them is emotionally upsetting. A, B and D are incorrect as they do not include any distressing answers.

27 The author explains how what she thought about the Anzacs was transformed by the personal information her grandfather shared with her about his grandfather's role in the war. A is incorrect because, although the author is pleased to learn something that links her with the Monster petition, she was already impressed with its story and it doesn't change her understanding. C and D are incorrect because there is no evidence of any better understanding emerging.

28 The author describes the task of collecting 30 000 signatures as 'herculean', a word derived from the name of the Roman God Hercules, famed for his strength. B, C and D are incorrect as they do not include similar adjectives.

29 The author provides examples to persuade the reader of the validity of his personal view that 'true alluvial gold is not always derived from the disintegration of lodes or reefs'. A and C are incorrect because the authors assume people today share their viewpoints. B is incorrect because it explains how a viewpoint has changed instead of trying to persuade anyone of its validity.

30 The Monster petition that was delivered to Parliament was the largest petition in the world at that time and it influenced women's gaining of the right to vote. B and C are incorrect because they do not refer to world records. D is incorrect because, although it refers to the discovery of the largest nugget of gold ever found at the time, there is no evidence that this discovery influenced politics.

READING TEST 2   Page 8

1 B   2 A   3 D   4 B   5 A   6 C   7 B   8 C   9 C
10 A   11 D   12 A   13 B   14 C   15 C   16 E
17 F   18 G   19 B   20 D   21 C   22 A   23 D
24 B   25 C   26 B   27 D   28 A   29 C   30 A

1 The events during Mr Brocklehurst's visit to a schoolroom, such as his complaints about the students' laundry use, food consumption and appearance, as well as Jane's carelessness, are similar although some of the details are different. A is incorrect because they are not about different events. C and D are incorrect because the texts are not identical or indistinguishable; the laundry complaint is about 'tuckers' in Text 1 but 'undies' in Text 2, for example.

2 You can work out that the narrator in Text 1 is Jane Eyre. She reports the conversations in the schoolroom and then speaks in the first person ('I might have escaped …'). In Text 2 Jane, although she doesn't speak, is a character who is punished for dropping her slate. This means B, C and D are incorrect.

3 You can judge that Mr Brocklehurst's behaviour is arrogant (he acts as though he is superior in every way), ignorant (he fails to recognise red, curly hair can be natural) and cruel (he takes pleasure in causing the students to suffer). He never displays any sign of humility. This makes A, B and C incorrect.

4 You can work out that at first Miss Temple tries to do as Mr Brocklehurst demands but as his requests become more unreasonable, she finds it difficult to respond to him. A is incorrect because there is no evidence in the text to indicate she has a sore throat. C is incorrect because she disapproves of Mr Brocklehurst's behaviour. This can be seen when she whispers kind words to Jane. D is incorrect because her obedience comes not from admiration but because it is forced from her against her will.

5 The author of Text 2 further exaggerates the already extreme behaviour described in Text 1 to turn it from drama to comedy. B is incorrect because everything is made more ridiculous and extreme, not less so. C and D are incorrect because neither imagery nor monologue are used for purposes of satire in Text 2.

6 The rhymes in Text 2 are designed to be lighthearted and amusing: undies/Sundays (the day of the week is pronounced in the British way), fate/slate, code/episode, for example. A, B and D are incorrect as the scene is not aiming to be serious, mysterious or persuasive.

7 You can judge that the main purpose of Text 1 is to expose the injustice of a system that allows students to be treated in humiliating and cruel ways. Text 2 highlights the injustice of that same system by showing it in an even more ridiculous light. A and C are incorrect because neither text is about hopefulness or dishonesty. D is incorrect because there is no mention of bravery in Text 1 and, while Miss Temple's words to Jane might be considered brave, they are not said directly to Mr Brocklehurst, which makes them less so.

8 Jane is the central focus of both texts. By changing Jane's surname from Eyre to Fair, the author of Text 2 is playing up her role as victim and turning her into a fair-haired heroine of a melodrama. A is incorrect because the names are linked through rhyme and so are not unrelated. B is incorrect because, although the name Jane Fair rhymes with or echoes the name Jane Eyre, the relationship between the names is more complex than this. D is incorrect because the names are different so they are not a direct copy of each other.

9 It was the attraction of the current craze of the bicycle that Mulga Bill found irresistible. A is incorrect because he had ridden for a long time so was likely to be at least competent. B is incorrect because there is no evidence that he didn't want to ride a horse in town. D is incorrect because undoubtedly he would like to show off as it is in his nature but there are many ways to do this—it was the new craze that he was 'caught' by.

10 'A man who blows' is someone who boasts or blows his own trumpet. This is what Mulga Bill denies he does, while doing exactly that: 'I'm good all round at everything'. B is incorrect because Mulga Bill is far from

modest and never shy. C is incorrect because, although he does seem keen to take part in things, his boastfulness is much more central to his character. D is incorrect because, while his behaviour may appear reckless when his bicycle bolts away, this is not what he wants to happen or how he means to behave.

11 The language used to describe the bicycle's journey to the creek is related to how a horse moves: it bolts, bounds, springs, races, bucks and swerves. A, B and C are incorrect because these actions are not typical of the movements of people, wallaroos or wombats.

12 You can judge that, in the context of the poem, the image of a chalk-white Mulga Bill being catapulted towards the creek with the natural world speedily removing itself from his path is primarily comical. B is incorrect because it is the comedy of the narrative that is emphasised and, while you might feel a moment of sympathy for Mulga Bill's plight, there is no tragedy. C and D are incorrect because, while Mulga Bill may be both frightened and bewildered, the picture created for the reader is chaotically amusing.

13 The rhythm carries the narrative forward in a rush as dramatic events pile up at quite a pace. A is incorrect because the forward impetus of the rhythm is not compatible with moving around aimlessly. C and D are incorrect because there is nothing stealthy or reflective about the rhythm of the poem.

14 Mulga Bill behaves with 'lordly pride' and overestimates his abilities from the outset. The inevitable result is his fall—literally— into Dead Man's Creek. A is partly true in that the poem is about a failed attempt at following a craze but this is seen as Mulga Bill's failure and it is not the moral of the poem which makes it incorrect. B is incorrect because Mulga Bill's claims are not so much untruths as pride or belief in his own accomplishments. D is incorrect because this theme is not explored in the poem.

15 In the previous sentence the author names Elizabeth's parents. This sentence gives further information about her father, Samuel: Her father, an innkeeper, died a few months after she was born. The sentence that follows tells about the will Samuel left when he died.

16 In the previous sentence the author is talking about when Elizabeth married and the name of her husband. This sentence tells where they lived: They set up home in London's East End near the Docks. The sentence that follows gives information about a significant event that took place early in their marriage when her husband was given command of the *Endeavour*.

17 In the previous sentence the author is talking about the death of one of their sons. This sentence adds the information that two more of their sons also died young: Their other two sons, James and Hugh, died before they had children of their own. The sentence that follows tells us the whole family died before Elizabeth did.

18 In the previous sentence the author is talking about Elizabeth's embroidery skills. This sentence describes an example of her work in more detail: An embroidered map sampler outlines her husband's three voyages to the Pacific. The sentence that follows tells where this sampler is kept today.

19 In the previous sentence the author is talking about the vest Elizabeth was embroidering for James while he was returning home. This sentence tells what she hoped he would do with her gift: She planned to give it to him to wear at court after his return. The sentence that follows gives more information about what the vest was made from and where it is now.

20 In the previous sentence the author describes a gift of a box the sailors gave to Elizabeth after James was killed. This sentence tells what she did with this box: She used it to store a tiny painting of Cook and a lock of his hair. The sentence that follows explains what her depth of feeling for her husband caused her to do before she died.

Note: The unused sentence is A.

21 The colts are hit and wounded when Dick, a plowboy, throws stones and sticks to make them gallop. A is incorrect because several poachers kill the giraffes. B is incorrect because the hunting of seals is not done by a human. D is incorrect because the death of the snails is mainly caused by other snails.

22 The radio program reports Ahmed Noor's actual words about using a GPS tracking device on the last white giraffe. B and D are incorrect because neither includes spoken words. C is incorrect because, although it includes words that are spoken, they are not said by conservationists.

23 You can judge that the research into why the *Partula hyaline* survived better than other snails led to the discovery that protecting forest-edge habitats may further assist their survival. A is incorrect because, although it is about a human intervention (adding a tracking system to the giraffe's horn), it is not known whether this was successful in keeping the last white giraffe alive. B is incorrect because human intervention is not described. C is incorrect because, although human intervention takes place, it is not related to the survival of a species.

24 You can work out that humans endangered sea lions by over-hunting them in the 19th century. A and D are incorrect as they discuss more recent events. C is incorrect because it is not about an animal species being endangered by human behaviour.

25 You can work out that, as this text is written in the first person as though spoken by a horse, it must be fictional. A, B and D are incorrect as they are factual rather than fictional texts.

26 From a distance, the large males with their orange-coloured ruffs of hair would have looked just like male lions to sailors, a likely explanation for their nickname 'lions of the sea'. A and C are incorrect as they do not include nicknames. D is incorrect because rosy wolf snail is its common name not its nickname.

27 You can work out that the smallest computer in the world represents a modern technology. It is attached to the snails with an everyday item: glue. A is incorrect because, although GPS tracking is also an example of a modern technology, it is not linked to an everyday item. B and C are incorrect because they do not refer to modern technologies.

28 You can judge that the white giraffe is the closest to extinction of any of the species described. B and D are incorrect because, although eared seals and the *Partula hyaline* are endangered species, they are not as close to extinction as the white giraffe. C is incorrect because colts are not endangered.

29 The master dismisses the boy for his cruelty, which means he is without a worker and has to find other help. A is incorrect because, although Ahmed responds to cruelty by having a tracker fitted to the giraffe's horn, this is not personally inconvenient for him. B is incorrect because personal inconvenience is not mentioned. D is incorrect because, although the researchers may have experienced personal inconvenience in their work, it is not referred to in this text.

30 Lack of pigmentation from leucism, a physical condition, removes much of the white giraffe's ability to find camouflage, making it vulnerable to attack. B is incorrect because it is the appearance of the seals from a distance that may have attracted hunters, not some physical defect. C is incorrect because it does not refer to a physical condition suffered by the horses. D is incorrect because the snails are described as becoming less vulnerable, not more so, and this is related to their physical qualities rather than to a rare defect.

READING TEST 3   Page 15

1 D 2 B 3 C 4 D 5 B 6 A 7 B 8 D 9 B
10 A 11 B 12 C 13 D 14 C 15 D 16 A
17 B 18 F 19 C 20 G 21 C 22 D 23 B
24 A 25 C 26 B 27 B 28 C 29 D 30 B

1 You can work out that what happened to Miss Morstan's missing father and the mysterious consequences that follow remain unsolved and that who stole the Diamond remains a mystery. A is incorrect because there is no evidence the pearls Miss Morstan receives are stolen. B is incorrect because, while the nature of police work can be observed, it is not what either text is mainly about. C is incorrect because, while Sherlock Holmes's fame as an investigator may be well known, Sergeant Cuff does not have a similar reputation.

2 You can work out that Holmes uses reason to come to conclusions about the letter he is shown and Cuff deduces how a theft can be solved by looking at a smear of paint. A is incorrect as Holmes's colleagues are not mentioned and Cuff finds his colleague unhelpful. C and D are incorrect because there is no evidence in the texts that either investigator uses shock tactics or underhand behaviour.

3 The clue that is investigated in Text 2 is a paint smear. A is incorrect because no dogs were present in the room where the smear occurred. B is incorrect because there was no handprint on the smear. D is incorrect because, although clothing may have brushed against the smear, it is the smear itself which provides that information.

4 The clue Holmes investigates by examining it closely is a letter. A is incorrect because, although Holmes notices a thumbprint on the letter, he does not investigate it at this stage. B and C are incorrect because, although Holmes is told about a pearl and a cardboard box, he does not investigate them at this stage.

5 Cuff uses polite sarcasm to insult his colleague, Superintendent Seegrave, when he takes over the case and sends him back to town. A, B and C are incorrect as there is no mention of Holmes's colleague.

6 You can judge that Miss Morstan does not allow her emotions to intrude into her account of what has happened. B and C are incorrect as she is both articulate and controlled in her telling of what has happened. D is incorrect because, although Miss Morstan shows every sign of being trustworthy, her role in the case has not yet been established so it is uncertain whether or not the word applies to her.

7 Sergeant Cuff is very sure of his own powers and contemptuous of those of his Sergeant. A, C and D are incorrect as the Inspector shows himself to be efficient, thorough and logical in the methods he uses to analyse the case.

8 You can judge that the word 'trifle' refers to the clue provided by the paint on the wall. It is also referred to as the 'mischief'. A is incorrect because there is no reward involved. B is incorrect because, although the trifle may have been caused by the brushing of a loose article against the wall, it is not the trifle itself. C is incorrect because the dogs' tails did not brush the wall or cause what Sergeant Cuff's colleague had thought but a trifle.

9 The narrator is spellbound by the stars just like someone who is 'star struck', or in awe of a celebrity. These galaxies are her world. A and D are incorrect because, although she may hope to be an astronomer or visit a star, this is not what it means to be 'a star-struck galaxy gazer'. C is incorrect because there is evidence in the text that she looks away from the telescope at times.

10 The comment that she should 'come down to earth' implies she thinks her sister spends too much time lost in space and should change her ways. B, C and D are incorrect as there is no evidence in the text that she approves, is uninterested in or admires what her sister does.

11 You can work out that a 'black hole' is a metaphor suggesting her brother's room is full of junk—a mess where nothing can be found and where what goes in never comes out. If you know that a black hole in space is a place with such strong gravitational pull that nothing ever comes out of it, you will understand this works as a further metaphor reinforcing the concept. A, C and D are incorrect because the description is a metaphor and not about the colour of the room, where it is located or how hard it is to find.

12 You can work out that the word 'milky' refers to the milky way, a galaxy of stars, but also to things becoming more obscure in her life, which can make her feel a bit lost. A, B and D are incorrect because there is no evidence in the text that the moon is shining through the stars, that her telescope has turned everything white or that the stars look misty.

13 You can judge that the last two lines are about a moment the narrator shares with her brother: they are both gripped by a similar dream and the spaces suggest they are moving slowly into this dreamlike state. A is incorrect because the rhythm slows down rather than speeds up. B is incorrect because it is clear the poem is ending without the spaces being included. C is incorrect because, while it seems her brother is a dreamer, the spaces suggest the moment is shared between the two of them dreaming together.

14 The poem explores the narrator's point of view about the wonder of exploring space, which one of her brothers shares but which her sister and other brother don't value in the same way. A is incorrect because it provides a literal definition of a horizon but doesn't tell what the poem is about. B is incorrect because the poem is not simply about what you can see from a telescope. D is incorrect because the idea that the sky is the limit is not explored.

15 In the previous sentence the author is talking about how a Japanese publisher introduced Japanese folktales to western readers. This sentence tells how he went about producing them: He printed a series of volumes that used the work of western writers and translators combined with brightly coloured original woodblock prints by noted Japanese artists. The sentence that follows describes which western readers were the readers of his books.

16 In the previous sentence the author tells how a boy was born from a peach in the tale *Little Peachling*. This sentence tells about his parents and his upbringing: His parents bring him up lovingly and he grows up to be strong, brave and generous hearted. The sentence that follows refers to the adventures he had as a young man and his care for his parents.

17 In the previous sentence the author is talking about a possible link between *Little Peachling* and the book *James and the Giant Peach*. This sentence adds a bracketed aside providing an anecdote about the origin of Dahl's story: (The story was originally going to be about a giant cherry but Dahl changed it to a peach because it is 'prettier, bigger and squishier than a cherry'.) The sentence that follows points out some of the main differences between the two stories.

18 In the previous sentence the author tells us a little about the boy in the story *The Boy who Drew Cats*. This sentence adds information about his passion for drawing cats: He loved to draw and from morning to evening, if you came across him anywhere, he'd probably be drawing cats. The sentence that follows tells how his love of drawing cats led to his expulsion from a monastery!

19 In the previous sentence the author refers to a temple, the home of an evil goblin rat, where the boy takes shelter. This sentence describes how the boy behaves after he gets there: After drawing cats on some screens in a room in the temple, he goes to sleep in a nearby cupboard. The sentence that follows reveals that when he wakes he finds the evil goblin rat dead on the floor and blood on the mouths of the cats he'd drawn earlier.

20 In the previous sentence the author comments that Japanese tales, in the format Hasegawa produced, are not viable in modern times. This sentence explains some reasons for this: Books like Hasegawa's series are too time-consuming and expensive to make today. The sentence that follows refers to other art forms that are currently responsible for spreading Japanese culture around the globe.

Note: The unused sentence is E.

21 The seasons and the garden act as though they are human in the selfish giant's world. The seasons choose whether or not to appear and the trees have feelings and use their branches as arms. A is incorrect because the settings for the sculptures are described realistically. B and D are incorrect as the natural world is not described in any detail.

22 You can work out that Robert Wadlow, a very tall human being, is noted for his kind and gentle nature and is well liked by others. A is incorrect because the Forgotten Giants are not alive so aren't human. B is incorrect because, while it is uncertain whether or not Goliath is a human or a 'real' giant in this story, he behaves in an aggressive, unfriendly way towards others. C is incorrect because the Selfish Giant is a storybook figure and is mainly unfriendly.

23 You can judge that Goliath scares an entire army by using his formidable size and his weapons in a threatening way. A is incorrect because the Forgotten Giants are inanimate and harmless. C is incorrect because, although the Giant's selfish behaviour affects his surroundings and those in them, he is less threatening than Goliath. D is incorrect because Robert is not at all scary.

24 The Forgotten Giants are placed in out of the way places to encourage people to visit them. B, C and D are incorrect as the giants in these texts do not encourage people to visit unfamiliar places.

25 You can judge that the Selfish Giant is the most likely of the giants to feel shame because he comes to understand the error of his ways. A is incorrect because the Forgotten Giants don't have feelings. B is incorrect because Goliath doesn't have time to feel anything about his behaviour after he is shot dead. D is incorrect because Robert doesn't do anything that would make him feel ashamed.

26 You can work out that battles between the Israelites and the Philistines took place a long time ago as Saul was the first king of the Israelites. (You may also know that the David and Goliath story comes from the Bible.) A is incorrect as the Forgotten Giants are placed in the modern, environmentally friendly city of Copenhagen. C is incorrect because, although the Selfish Giant may be from a story told long ago, it appears to be timeless as there is no indication of its time frame. D is incorrect because Robert lived in the early 20th century, which is long after the founding of Israel.

27 You can judge that Goliath is a bully as he repeats his frightening threats day after day and is ready to kill the seemingly vulnerable David. A and D are incorrect as these 'giants' are not bullies. C is incorrect because, although the Selfish Giant may be capable of being a bully, we don't learn about him threatening anyone.

28 The Selfish Giant's heart is said to melt as something hard and solid can melt when it is warmed. This means his heart softens and he feels kindly towards the children. A, B and D do not include metaphors that describe a heart's behaviour.

29 When Robert Wadlow says he 'overlooks' those who stare at him, he is making a 'punny' joke! He uses the word to mean both that he ignores them and that he looks over the top of them because of his height. A, B and C do not include jokes.

30 You can judge that David's unexpectedly instant success with his inferior size and weaponry against Goliath is the sudden climax to which the story builds. A is incorrect because the account doesn't build to a climax. C is incorrect because, although it records the giant's transformation which is the climax of the story, it is described slowly and methodically rather than suddenly. D is incorrect because, although it may be surprising that there are scale models of Robert around the world, this fact is not built towards in the telling and is more of a conclusion than a climax.

READING TEST 4   Page 21

1 C **2** B **3** A **4** B **5** D **6** B **7** C **8** B **9** B
10 A **11** B **12** D **13** B **14** C **15** B **16** G
17 D **18** F **19** E **20** C **21** B **22** D **23** A
24 B **25** D **26** B **27** C **28** A **29** B **30** D

1 In Text 1 the narrator is recalling a time when she was 'barely three' and in Text 2 the narrator is recalling a time when she was seven years old. A, B and D are incorrect because these themes occur in only one text, not both: Text 2 is about a quarrel and promises while Text 1 is about danger.

2 The narrator's tears are caused by hot embers that burn her fists when she picks up her father's pipe. A, C and D are incorrect because none of these things happen in the text.

3 You can work out that the gum trees, the gurgling fern-banked stream, the scrubby hill and the gold diggings with its mullocks are typical of an Australian landscape. B and C are incorrect as Text 2 is not set in a

particular landscape. D is incorrect because Text 1 is set in an Australian landscape.

4 The powerful emotional cruelty caused by her playmate is stamped forever in the narrator's memory. She says it has become part of 'my inmost fibre'. A is incorrect because the memory the narrator recalls in Text 1 is the physical experience of pain: getting burnt on her hands. C and D are incorrect because emotional pain is only recalled in one text.

5 You can work out that the narrator and her father share a close bond in Text 1. He often takes her with him as he works; he protects her, comforts her when she is hurt and understands her ways. A, B and C are incorrect because there is nothing overpowering, distant or awkward in their relationship.

6 You can judge that the narrator of Text 1 is confident and assertive at times, whereas the narrator of Text 2 finds it difficult to stand up for herself. A is incorrect because, although the narrators are both recalling memories from their childhood, their characters are quite different. C and D are incorrect because the narrators are of different ages (three and seven) and the backgrounds they recall are very different (the outback and the yard behind a house).

7 The narrator cannot recall what the girl was named but she can recall she wore a Stuart plaid frock so she uses this detail to identify her. A is incorrect because the girl did not say this was her name. B is incorrect because, although Stuart plaid is of Scottish origin, this doesn't mean the girl is Scottish. D is incorrect because, although it is true she detested the girl and this may have unconsciously influenced her choice of such an unattractive name, it is not the reason given for her choice.

8 You can judge that Stuart plaid's motivation is to make it seem as though her destruction of the tea-things was caused by the narrator breaking their agreement to swap. A is incorrect because she didn't want to return the tea-things. C is incorrect because there was no need to start a new quarrel as they were engaged in one already. D is incorrect because, although the effect of her words is to show how nasty she can be, her aim is to make it seem as though it is the narrator's fault.

9 The line emphasises the similarities between the snake and the narrator: they are both doing the same thing for the same reason at the same place. A is incorrect because the line does more than show why they are at the water trough; it shows they have similar needs and they do similar things. C is incorrect because the line is not related to the size of the trough. D is incorrect because, while it is true it is hot, this is not emphasised by the line.

10 The narrator has been brought up to wait his turn; it is an automatic response to stand and wait when someone arrives before him. B is incorrect because his decision to wait is motivated by learned behaviour and is not an impulse. C is incorrect because there is no suggestion at this stage of the poem that he feels afraid. D is incorrect because, although he does become fascinated by the snake, at this stage he has only just noticed it.

11 He throws the log at the snake because he listens to the voice of education that lives in his head: venomous snakes are dangerous and must be killed. A is incorrect because no-one tells him to harm the snake. C and D are incorrect because, although he may have been taught these things, it is not why he throws the log at the snake.

12 The narrator regrets the pettiness of trying to harm an animal so dignified and part of the natural world. A is incorrect because he wishes he hadn't tried to hit the snake. B is incorrect because this doesn't occur to him. C is incorrect because with hindsight he knows he didn't want to kill the snake.

13 You can work out that the narrator is ashamed of what he did. He did not listen to what the experience showed him: that here was a magnificent creature worthy of admiration and wonder. A, C and D are incorrect because he doesn't blame anything or anyone other than himself.

14 You can judge that respect is the dominant feeling the narrator holds towards the snake. His attitude changes but underlying it for the most part is a kind of admiration that earns his respect. A is incorrect because, although the narrator allows a moment of fear to sway his attitude, it is not his most dominant feeling. B and D are incorrect because there is no evidence the narrator experiences feelings of dislike or love for the snake.

15 In the previous sentence the author is talking about the ship that Arnhem Land was named after. This sentence tells who sailed that ship: It sailed into the Gulf of Carpentaria in 1623 under the leadership of a captain of the Dutch East India Company. The sentence that follows adds that the name, Arnhem Land, was made official after 1931.

16 In the previous sentence the author gives the information that it has been populated by Indigenous people for centuries. This sentence gives information about the current population: Today it has a small population of around 18 000 people. The sentence that follows explains that many of these people are local Yolngu people.

17 In the previous sentence the author refers to the need for a permit. This sentence tells when to apply for the permit: It needs to be applied for about two weeks in advance. The sentence that follows is about permit costs.

18 In the previous sentence the author gives a general description of the landscape of Arnhem Land. This sentence gives more details about its nature: Unspoilt wilderness and stone country with rugged escarpments and magnificent ancient rainforests are part of its landscape. The sentence that follows supplies further details of the features that characterise its land.

19 In the previous sentence the author refers to the need for a permit. This sentence tells when to apply for the permit: It needs to be applied for about two weeks in advance. The sentence that follows is about permit costs.

20 In the previous sentence the author tells where you can find examples of the x-ray art form. This sentence gives details of what is revealed in the paintings: The paintings include the internal organs and bones of their subjects. The sentence that follows gives

further information about the nature of the details included in these images.

Note: The unused sentence is A.

21 You can work out that the common name of the axolotl, the Mexican walking fish, is surprising since a characteristic of a fish is that it cannot walk. A, C and D are incorrect as they do not include surprising names for the subjects of their research.

22 Environmentally friendly disposal of plastic is a worldwide problem and it is stated that recent research into the waxworm may lead the way to a promising solution. A is incorrect because the problem being researched is not serious and there are plenty of solutions available. B is incorrect because, although it is implied that research might lead to a better understanding of tissue regeneration, this intention is not stated. It is also unlikely that humans would be able to regenerate whole limbs. C is incorrect because research into the lyrebird's ability to imitate is not designed to rid the world of a serious problem.

23 The reports of cockatoos scavenging for 'takeaways' is told with humour and a lack of seriousness. B, C and D are incorrect as these texts are relatively serious in their presentation.

24 Amphibians live both on water and on land but the axolotl is an exception as it lives in water. A, C and D are incorrect because you can work out that cockatoos, lyrebirds and waxworms are not amphibians as they live only on land.

25 You can judge that this text makes greater use of technical terms, such as 'polyethylene', 'nonbiodegradable', 'microorganisms' and 'metabolise', than the other texts. A and C are incorrect as they use very few technical terms. B is incorrect because, although it uses some technical terms such as 'larva/larval' and 'amphibian', it doesn't use as many as D.

26 Researchers breed axolotls in captivity to provide the numbers they need. A, C and D are incorrect as they do not explain how animals are collected for researchers' studies.

27 Through its ability to imitate other sounds, the superb lyrebird can deceive listeners, including humans and birds from different species, into thinking they can hear things that are not there. A, B and D are about animals that don't use their abilities to deceive.

28 You can work out that cockatoos learn from copying other cockatoos. B, C and D are incorrect because the behaviour of these animals is a result of their genetic behaviour as a species, not something learned.

29 You can work out that being able to regenerate limbs and brain cells that are damaged or lost would transform the quality of an axolotl's life. A is incorrect because, although cockatoos are finding new ways to get food, this discovery will not transform their lives as other sources of food are available. C is incorrect because, although you could assume lyrebirds use imitation to attract a mate, this is not asserted in the text and is not as transforming as replacing a lost limb. D is incorrect because it is not about how waxworms use their abilities to improve their lives.

30 You can work out that if the waxworm's ability to dispose of plastic leads to successful ways to prevent plastic polluting the environment, then this could help transform our planet. A, B and C are incorrect because the abilities described are not likely to result in significant changes to our planet.

THINKING SKILLS Test 1   Page 27

1 B   2 B   3 A   4 A   5 C   6 D   7 B   8 A   9 D
10 C   11 C   12 D   13 B   14 D   15 A   16 A
17 D   18 B   19 C   20 B   21 C   22 B   23 A
24 A   25 A   26 A   27 C   28 D   29 D   30 C
31 A   32 D   33 D   34 D   35 B   36 B   37 D
38 A   39 C   40 C

1 The number of scoops purchased by the 13 students who did not order single scoops is given by: $47 - 12 = 35$. So 13 students purchased 35 scoops together. Some purchased 2 scoops and some purchased 3 scoops. You need to find two numbers that sum to 13 that you can put into the following number sentence:

[ ] × 2 + ( ) × 3 = 35. For example, 0 and 13: [0] × 2 + (13) × 3 ≠ 35. So 0 and 13 are not the answers. You can continue to look at 1 and 12, 2 and 11, etc. but they are not options. So the best thing to do is use the next given option. If 4 students ordered double scoops, then 9 students must have ordered triple scoops as 4 + 9 = 13 students. [4] × 2 + (9) × 3 = 35. So the answer is B.

2 The information in the box states that cassowaries 'will swim when they need to'. Daniel has correctly reasoned that the bird may be a cassowary that needs to get somewhere so will swim across the river to get to the other side.

3 The Jacaranda had grown 3.6 m in 9 years, giving a growth rate of 0.4 m per year. (4.6 − 1) ÷ 9 = 3.6 ÷ 9 = 0.4. Using the same method it can be shown that the growth rates of the other trees were higher.

The Spotted Gum: (2.9 − 1.4) ÷ 3 = 0.5

The Paper Bark: 2.5 ÷ 5 = 0.5

The Camphor Laurel: (7.7 − 2.2) ÷ 10
= 5.5 ÷ 10 = 0.55

4 Thomas was at 90 m when Alec completed the race. This means he was running at 90% of Alec's pace. Similarly, Christo was running at 90% of Thomas's pace. 0.9 × 0.9 = 0.81 That is, 90% of 90% is 81% which means Christo was running at 81% of the speed of Alec. When Alec completed the race, Christo was at 81 m. Now, 100 − 81 = 19. So Alec beat Christo by 19 m.

5 Freya is trying to convince the local council to implement a program to collect and recycle household food scraps because this will support the council's zero-waste target. The fact that recycling food scraps will save up to one third of household waste from ending up in landfill is a positive step towards the council achieving its zero-waste target so C strengthens Freya's argument.

6

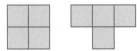

The other three solutions are shown below. Try cutting out the shapes from D and trying to make a square from them. It is not possible:

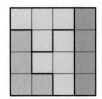
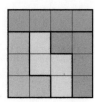
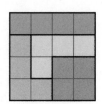

7 The change in the number of cards between the start of the day and the end is given by: 8 + 25 − 13 = 20. So they ended the day with 20 more cards than they started with. Take this from 65 to find how many they started with: 65 − 20 = 45. Now, each student started with the same number of cards: 45 ÷ 3 = 15. So each student must have started the day with 15 cards.

8 You need to work out which statement is not possible. You are told that if David does not practise his goal kicking, then his ability to kick goals won't improve. It cannot then be true that David didn't practise but his goal kicking improved.

9 You are told that people use chickpeas to make hummus. You are also told that chickpeas are pulses and that you have to cook pulses before eating them. From the information given, you can conclude that hummus is made from cooked chickpeas.

10 Take a look at the 'Matches' row. Total number of matches in each competition is 127. So together they have 127 × 2 = 254 matches.

	Players	**Matches**
Round 1	128	64
Round 2	64	32
Round 3	32	16
Round 4	16	8
Quarterfinal	8	4
Semifinal	4	2
Final	2	1
Total		127

11 You need to decide which sentence is a conclusion you could draw from the information and is therefore true. It must be true that if the team is two goals ahead at half time, Hans will be allowed on the field but only as goalie for some time in the second half while the team remains two goals ahead.

12

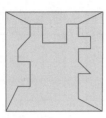

13

It is possible for all others by moving the grey circle:

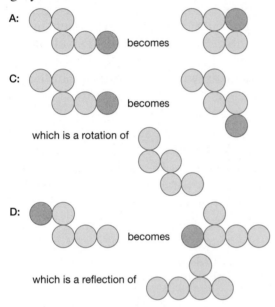

A:

becomes

C:

becomes

which is a rotation of

D:

becomes

which is a reflection of

It is impossible to move only one circle to create B.

14 You are told that any students who did not get selected for the volleyball team last term will be given the chance of selection this term. Bec uses incorrect reasoning when she says that because Marcus did not get selected last term, he will definitely want to be selected this term. Marcus might be further discouraged from trying out again this term for fear of a second rejection. He may also have enrolled in a different activity or he could have decided he's not interested in volleyball anymore. Bec cannot assert that Marcus will want to try out this term.

15 You need to identify the assumption that has led to the conclusion. Assumptions are correct if they are supported by evidence.

Evidence: Lauren announces she has an 8 am meeting in the city on Friday with a new client. Conclusion: Lauren needs to catch a very early bus to allow plenty of time to get to her meeting. Tobias has assumed the meeting is important.

16 Every tile is the same. The tiles only need to be rotated to complete the pattern.

17 Alejandro knows it's against the law for a pedestrian to cross a road against a flashing red light but he's never seen or heard of anyone getting caught and fined. Therefore he concludes that it's ok to break the law as long as you don't get caught.

18 Myumi uses correct reasoning. She acknowledges Ed's physical and mental skills. She also acknowledges Ed's liabilities: his finger injuries. Myumi says Ed has a great attitude and that will give him a good chance of success. Having a chance allows for the possibility that he won't be successful.

19 It is easy to think that the minute hand will meet the hour hand every hour and so will therefore pass it 12 times in 12 hours. However, the minute hand completes more than one revolution before meeting up with the hour hand each time. If you start at midnight, the hands will point in the same direction at approximately: 1:05, 2:11, 3:16, 4:22, 5:27, 6:33, 7:38, 8:44, 9:49, 10:54 and then exactly at 12 noon. This is 11 times in 12 hours. In 24 hours this is $11 \times 2 = 22$ times. In a single day, the minute hand will point in the same direction as the hour hand 22 times.

20 The main idea will be included somewhere in the text and will be supported by the rest of the information. The main idea is that, for optimum wellbeing, elderly people require physical and mental exercise and social interaction. In this text the main idea is expressed in the first sentence.

21 The information in the box tells you that everyone who likes scary movies/thrillers likes action/adventure movies and therefore (since they like action and adventure movies) they also like science fiction but not comedies. So it is reasonable to draw the conclusion that if Twyla likes scary movies/thrillers, she does not enjoy comedies.

22 Callan is one year older than Olive so he must be 10. Isla is five years older than Callan so she must be 15.

23 If this were a solution, the top view would have a line partway or all the way through the middle of the shape to signify the edge at the top of the solid.

24 The argument is that Landcare is an important volunteer movement that helps the environment while building cohesive communities. The statement that most strengthens the argument is that children can become involved in their communities through joining Landcare.

25 If any of his daughters has 2 sons or more, they will get to name a child after their father. Four of his daughters have at least 2 sons. If any of his sons have 1 son or more, they will get to name a child after their father. One of his sons has a son. He will have 4 + 1 = 5 grandchildren named after him.

26 This statement argues in support of the media using the word 'attack' and so weakens the argument in the text.

27 All dogs that chase their tail are good and Ned is a dog that chases his tail. Therefore he is a good dog. 1 and 2, and 3 and 4, do not tell us that Ned is a good dog. To see why this is true, change the statements slightly. If you change 1 and 2 to 'All Labradors are dogs' and 'Ned is a dog' you can see it does not necessarily make Ned a Labrador. It is for the same reason that 1 and 2, and 3 and 4, do not make Ned a good dog.

28 On day 2 I got sunburnt so I need to know whether I applied multiple layers of sunscreen because if I did, the claim of my valuable lesson is not true. On day 3 I applied multiple layers of sunscreen so I need to know whether I got sunburnt, because if I did, the claim of my valuable lesson is not true. So I need to know b and c.

29 If the tiger is behind Door 3, then the first statements on Doors 1 and 3 must be true and the two statements on Door 2 must be false. As exactly 3 statements are true and 3 are false, one of the remaining statements must be true and one must be false. If the second statement on Door 1 is true, then the snake must be behind Door 2 but that would mean that the second statement on Door 3 is also true. If the second statement on Door 1 is false, then the snake must be behind Door 1 but that would mean the second statement on Door 3 is also false. This would mean that, if the tiger was behind Door 3, there cannot be 3 true statements and 3 false statements. So the tiger cannot be behind Door 3.

30 The medical practice has twice as many storeys as the sporting-goods store, which has two. Therefore the medical practice has four storeys and is situated at the far right of the row. The music store is one storey high and is immediately to the right of the book store. The sporting-goods store is two storeys high and is immediately to the right of the bank. Now, if the two end buildings are the same height and one of them is the medical practice at four storeys high, then the building at the other end must also be four storeys high. It can be either the bank or the book store, as the bank must be immediately to the left of the sporting-goods store and the book store must be immediately to the left of the music store. The last bit of information tells us the music store and the book store combine to equal the height of the bank. If the bank is on the end it is four storeys high and the book store must be three storeys high (three storeys plus one storey gives us four storeys).

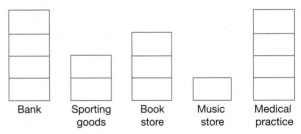

Bank   Sporting   Book   Music   Medical
        goods   store   store   practice

If the bookstore is on the end, it is four storeys high and the bank must be five storeys high and in the middle of the row:

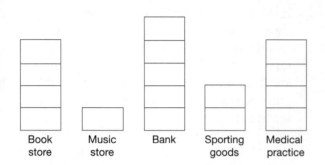

Book store | Music store | Bank | Sporting goods | Medical practice

The question tells us the bank is in the middle of the row. Therefore the book store must be four storeys high.

31 The second and fourth pieces of information tell us if Anika makes a large mistake, she will not make a good-quality cabinet and that without a good-quality cabinet she has no chance of winning the prize. She cannot win the prize without a good-quality cabinet.

32 The first and third pieces of information tell us all those who like draughts also like chess and some who like draughts also like backgammon. If a student likes backgammon and draughts, they must also like chess. You know that some students like backgammon and draughts. Therefore D is the statement that cannot be true.

33 Lucy has understood you can earn one free smoothie for every five smoothies purchased and so she reasons correctly that ten smoothie purchases earn two free smoothies.

34 For the garlic to be large and flavoursome, it needs to **both** have been planted on the shortest day of the year **and** harvested on the longest day of the year. If it is neither large nor flavoursome, this means it was either not planted on the shortest day of the year or it was not harvested on the longest day of the year. It could also have not been planted on the shortest day as well as not harvested on the longest day. However, we don't know which of these scenarios is the case. While the conclusions of both gardeners **might** be true, they are not necessarily true from the information given.

35 Read Raphael's argument and then judge which statement weakens his argument. There would be circumstances where, if you love an animal, you would condone putting it down because you don't want it to suffer.

36 The question tells us we must accept all the statements are true. As Keegan's statement is true, if he does not skate at his best he will not win a medal. He is saying the **only** way he can win a medal is if he skates at his best. He won a medal so he must have skated at his best.

Pedro's statement is also true ('If I land every trick, I will win a medal.') but he is not saying the only way he can win a medal is by landing every trick. For example, it may also be true that if Pedro lands the best trick but stacks some others, he will win a medal. That is, landing every trick is **not necessarily the only way** Pedro will win a medal. So A is not necessarily true.

The same logic applies to Rune's statement.

37 The information tells us a successful restaurant must have good customer service. Millie's Restaurant does not have good customer service so it cannot be successful. The other options are all possible but they are not necessarily true. For A, it might be true that there is a third condition: that a restaurant needs to be reasonably priced to be successful. It might be that Millie's Restaurant does not have reasonable prices and so is not successful even though it has good service and tasty food. For B, Millie's Restaurant might serve tasty food but not have good service. For C, Millie's Restaurant might have good service but might not serve tasty food.

38 Blake has concluded that if you don't eat meat, you will be unhealthy. For Blake's conclusion to hold, it must be assumed that meat is the only way people get protein in their diet. Remember: Evidence (E) + Assumption (A) = conclusion (C).

(E: If you don't get enough protein, you will be unhealthy + A: Meat is the only way people get protein in their diet = C: If you don't eat meat, you will be unhealthy.)

39 The main idea is expressed in the final sentence of the text: that pumpkin is a very versatile vegetable. The rest of the information supports this main idea by giving examples of the use of pumpkin in a variety of sweet or savoury dishes.

40 Jennifer is faster than Marion, who is faster than Simone. Isabella is faster than Simone. Cathy is faster than Isabella, who is faster than Simone. Everyone is faster than Simone so she must come fifth and not fourth. All the other answers are possible.

THINKING SKILLS Test 2

Page 37

1 D   2 D   3 B   4 A   5 B   6 C   7 C   8 C   9 A
10 D   11 C   12 D   13 B   14 B   15 A   16 D
17 B   18 D   19 C   20 D   21 A   22 B   23 B
24 A   25 A   26 B   27 B   28 B   29 C   30 D
31 B   32 C   33 A   34 A   35 D   36 A   37 B
38 C   39 A   40 C

1 When a cog's teeth engage with another's, the cogs spin in the opposite direction. If two cogs are attached by a belt as the two below are, they will spin in the same direction. The top-left gear is spinning in a clockwise direction. The cog that holds 1 and 2 will spin in an anticlockwise direction, while the cog that holds 3 and 4 will spin in a clockwise direction. This means 1 and 4 will go down while 2 and 3 will go up.

2 This statement cannot be true because you have been told that any player who has played half or more of the possible home and away games with teams in higher grades will not be allowed to play in finals games in a lower grade. Imogen has played seven of twelve games with the A team so she cannot play in the B-team finals.

3 The four and the three must be on opposite sides as they add up to seven. They cannot both be seen when looking at a standard six-sided dice.

4 There are five Thursdays in December 2022 and four in January 2023. Christmas Day, Boxing Day and New Year's Day all fall on Bridge Club days. The days on which bridge is played are:
December: 1, 4, 5, 11, 12, 15, 18, 19, 29
January: 2, 5, 8, 9, 15, 16, 19, 22, 23, 29, 30.
The club meets on 20 days altogether.

December						
Sun.	Mon.	Tue.	Wed.	Thu.	Fri.	Sat.
				1	2	3
4	5	6	7	8	9	10
11	12	13	14	15	16	17
18	19	20	21	22	23	24
25	26	27	28	29	30	31

January						
Sun.	Mon.	Tue.	Wed.	Thu.	Fri.	Sat.
1	2	3	4	5	6	7
8	9	10	11	12	13	14
15	16	17	18	19	20	21
22	23	24	25	26	27	28
29	30	31				

5 In this text the main idea is expressed in the second sentence. The main idea is that Cleopatra was a strong and powerful ruler in a male-dominated era. The rest of the information supports this main idea by providing further information and supporting evidence.

6 There were 20 animals altogether. Five were the glizzos so the plinkers and blippos make up 15 animals. $20 - 5 = 15$. There was one more plinker than blippo so the only option is eight plinkers and seven blippos. $8 + 7 = 15$. The number of legs that the plinkers and blippos had is 46: $(8 \times 4) + (7 \times 2) = 46$. The number of legs that the five glizzos had is 30: $76 - 46 = 30$. Each glizzo had 6 legs: $30 \div 5 = 6$.

7 From the diagram you can see that, after following the pattern for 33 km, Aaron is standing 3 km east of his starting position. Therefore to return he must head west for 3 km.

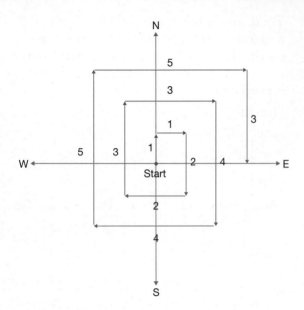

8   You are told that children preferred yellow to blue and purple, and that they liked green less than purple, red equal to purple and green more than orange. You can work out that the cubby house will be painted yellow.

9   The argument is that wire fences, especially barbed-wire fences, are dangerous for wildlife so any statement that gives a reason **for** installing barbed wire weakens the argument **against** it.

10 A: Terrence has three of a kind of an odd number. This must be true. A pair of any number will sum to an even number. Three of a kind of an even number will sum to an even number. The only way to get an odd sum on all five dice is to have three of a kind of an odd number.

B: Terrence scored 21 and the dice showed two 6s. This might be true. Three 3s and two 6s gives a total of 21.

C: The difference between the sum of the pair and the sum of the three of a kind is 1. This might be true. If Terrence rolled 5, 5, 3, 3, 3, the sum of the pair (5 + 5) is 10 and the sum of the three of a kind (3 + 3 + 3) is 9. The difference between the two is 1.

D: Terrence scored 19 and has no 5s. This cannot be true. To score 19, Terrence must either roll 5, 5, 3, 3, 3 or 2, 2, 5, 5, 5. Both options include a 5.

11 Neither Aran nor Nikita show correct reasoning. Aran is incorrect when he says Gabriella would make an excellent nurse because Gabriella has stated that she wants to be a writer. There's no information to support an assumption that Gabriella even wants to be a nurse. Nikita is incorrect in assuming that Nazeem can overcome his phobia of blood and become a great nurse just because he is compassionate and has excellent communication skills. There is no information in the box to support the assumption that Nazeem even wants to be a nurse.

12 If the spades are dealt out evenly, keeping the number of cards each player receives to a minimum, three players will have three spades and one player must have four. No matter how they are dealt, one player must have at least four spades. A might be true but it is possible for a player to receive no hearts. B might be true but it is not always the case. C also might be true as all 13 hearts might be dealt to one player.

13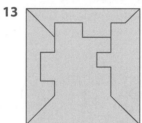

14 For someone to have taken the dog they must have had both the time and a good reason, so anyone who did not have the time or a good reason couldn't have been the one that took the dog. B is correct because if Yvette didn't have a good reason, she could not have taken the dog.

15 The argument is that farmers understand the importance of action to prevent climate change and are working to mitigate its effects. The statement that most strengthens the argument is that farmers are playing a vital role in ensuring resilience to climate change in rural areas.

16 When no torches are lit there is one message:

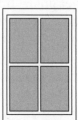

When one torch is lit it can be in any of the four windowpanes so there are four possible messages:

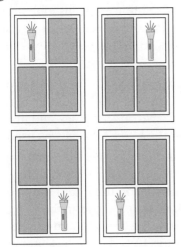

When two torches are lit there are six possible messages. Start with a torch at the top left and move the second torch around the other three windowpanes. Then put a torch at the top right and do the same, noting there are only two combinations as the combination that includes the top-left windowpane has already been counted. Then there is only one combination left when you start with a torch in the bottom-right corner:

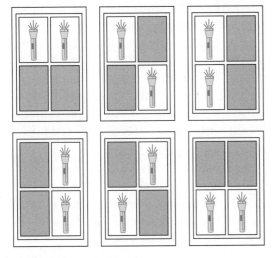

There are 11 different messages the friends can send.

17 Mariah's argument is that she feels lucky and so believes she is certain to win the lottery this week. B is correct because, although Mariah may feel lucky, she cannot be certain she will win the lottery. The lottery is a game of chance.

18 Both people are incorrect in their reasoning. Reggie says they **might** be about to experience an earthquake because his dog is unusually restless. He does not say there **will** be an earthquake so Brett is incorrect in saying that Reggie is wrong to claim his dog can predict an earthquake. Carly is incorrect to claim that Reggie has declared his dog is restless because it senses an earthquake is coming. Reggie has only said there **might** be an earthquake.

19 Martha can buy a maximum of 9 pizzas with $80. She can do this in any of three ways. First she could purchase 4 pizzas for $35 twice and then 1 pizza for $10: $35 + 35 + 10 = 80$. But she would get no change. Or she could purchase 4 pizzas for $35, 3 pizzas for $25 and then 2 pizzas for $18: $35 + 25 + 18 = 78$. Here she would get $2 in change: $80 - 78 = 2$. But her best option is to purchase three lots of 3 pizzas for $25: $25 + 25 + 25 = 75$. Her change would then be $5, as $80 - 75 = 5$.

20 The mistake Viktor has made is in not considering the fact that there may be other ways to win a free pass to the festival other than by answering at least five questions correctly or by submitting a self-recorded original piece of music. This is something that Viktor has not thought of so it is a flaw in his reasoning.

21 You can judge that conspiracy theorists are not always prepared to change their minds if they are shown scientific evidence. You are told that flat-earthers, for example, have firmly held beliefs and a mistrust of authorities. They have an answer for anything scientists can tell them or show them to prove the Earth is a sphere. It is not likely that scientific evidence will change their minds so based on the information you've been given, A cannot be true.

22 On Sunday Kristina completed 6 more than she did on Saturday. On Saturday she completed 5 more than she did on Friday. This pattern continues back to Monday. The number of extra push-ups Kristina did on Sunday compared to Monday is given by:

$$6 + 5 + 4 + 3 + 2 + 1 = (6+1) + (5+2) + (4+3)$$
$$= 3 \times 7$$
$$= 21$$
$$36 - 21 = 15$$

So Kristina completed 15 push-ups on Monday.

23 Takuma has assumed he must be the cause of Sean's short temper. Remember: Evidence (E) + Assumption (A) = Conclusion (C).

The evidence (E) is that Sean is very short-tempered with him. Takuma has assumed (A) that he is the cause of Sean's short temper when he draws this conclusion (C) and makes the decision to avoid Sean.

24 Let us assume only one artist submitted four artworks. If this is true then four artists submitted three artworks, as four times as many artists entered three artworks than four artworks and $1 \times 4 = 4$. This means 16 artists submitted one artwork, as $4 \times 4 = 16$.

If, instead, you assumed that two artists submitted four artworks, then eight artists must have submitted three artworks and 32 must have submitted one artwork. Together this is already 64 artworks, as $2 \times 4 + 8 \times 3 + 32 \times 1 = 64$, and you know only 52 were submitted. So only one person could have submitted four artworks and our first assumption is correct.

So the total number of artworks so far is given by:

$$\text{artworks so far} = 1 \times 4 + 4 \times 3 + 16 \times 1$$
$$= 4 + 12 + 16$$
$$= 32$$

That means there are 20 artworks submitted by artists who submitted two artworks: $52 - 32 = 20$. Therefore there are 10 artists who submitted two artworks: $20 \div 2 = 10$.

25 If the two work together for one hour, they will produce 60 products. One will produce 24 and the other will produce 36: $24 + 36 = 60$. The rate that products are produced together is now 60 per hour. This is 60 per 60 minutes. You can simplify this to 1 product per minute. In 25 minutes they will produce 25 products.

26 The argument not to sell peanut products at the fete is best supported by the statement that the school must ensure the health and safety of its students and put student wellbeing ahead of profits. This is a strong health-and-safety argument.

27 If Eva finishes in the top 10 regularly and those who finish in the top 20 regularly are considered elite, then Eva is considered elite. The third sentence tells us elite athletes train for over 15 hours every week but doesn't tell us those who do this are always considered elite.

28 If LUSH LAWN was used on Lawn 2, you need to know it produced a thick and lush lawn. If Lawn 3 is not thick and lush, you need to know if LUSH LAWN was used on it.

29 David and Olivia give the same answer. If either of them is the person telling the whole truth, then Jason did it and they both didn't. So both of them would make two true statements. Neither of them can be the person who always tells the truth. That person must be Jason and Olivia broke the table.

30 This option relies on the second and fourth sentences. If Hima injures herself, she **will not** train well. If she doesn't train well, she has **no chance** of winning. Therefore it is impossible for her to injure herself and still win the race. The key to answering this question is to look at which sentences use the word 'likely'. A, B and C might be unlikely but they are not impossible.

31 The first piece of information tells us for someone to like fantasy they must also like science-fiction. The third piece of information tells us no-one who likes romance likes science-fiction. So it is impossible for someone to like both fantasy and romance, as those who like fantasy must like science-fiction and those who like romance must not.

32 Heston has concluded that, because he played last weekend, he definitely won't play this weekend. His mistake is that just because the coach said someone who didn't have time on the field last weekend will definitely have time on the field this weekend, it does not mean that anyone who had time on the field last weekend will not have time on the field this weekend.

33 From the first piece of information given, you know the pianist is in Room 1 and the drummer is next door in Room 2 with a pizza. The bassist ordered a steak, the singer ordered a salad and the person who ordered soup was in Room 3. So you know the person

in Room 3 can't be the pianist, the drummer, the bassist or the singer, as the pianist and drummer are in Room 1 and Room 2, and the bassist and singer didn't order the soup. So the guitarist must be in Room 3 with the soup. You know from the information given that the guitarist is next to the bassist so the bassist must be in Room 4, as the drummer is in Room 2. This leaves the singer in Room 5 with a salad.

34 If Kayla is wrong then the sun was out. If Taran is right then the temperature was over 20 degrees Celsius. But you know from the information in the box that if the sun is out and the temperature is over 20 degrees then the washing will be dry after 4 hours. The washing was not dry so A is not possible. In B, C and D, at least one of the conditions for dry washing is not met. So dry washing cannot be guaranteed. For example, in B, Kayla is wrong and Taran is wrong. This means the sun was out but the temperature was not over 20 degrees. It is possible for these two things to be true and the washing not to be dry.

35 From the information given, it is not possible for Miles to have not been cycling well for some time and not to have given up cycling. He said that once he consistently stops enjoying cycling, he will give it up.

36 Create a table for the four friends and fill in the details as you read the information. You will have to read the information more than once. You can place Darlington and the car with Kevin and Penny straight away. The fact that the bike must go with Maroubra and that Toby did not go to Maroubra places the bike and Maroubra with Frederick. If you can't walk to Darlington, then Kevin must use the bus and Toby must walk. If you can't walk to Mosman, then Penny must travel to Mosman by car and Toby must walk to Glebe.

Person	Place	Transport
Kevin	Darlington	bus
Penny	Mosman	car
Frederick	Maroubra	bicycle
Toby	Glebe	walk

37 The third statement in the question has the same meaning as 'If you become an elite player, then you played against the best opposition'. That is, the **only** way to become an elite player is to play against the best opposition. Similarly, the fourth statement has the meaning that 'If you play for your country, you must be an elite player'. Taking these two statements together, it must be true that Patrick played against the best opposition. While the other options are possible, they are not necessarily true. Patrick may not have trained hard but could have been selected for another team that played against the best opposition.

38 In this text the main idea is expressed in the first sentence: that Internet scams are big business with people around the world losing billions of dollars to scammers. The rest of the information supports this main idea by providing further information and supporting evidence.

39 The statement that weakens the argument is that the best zoos give their animals antidepressant medication. The best zoos would not need to give animals antidepressants because those zoos would have prevented their animals suffering from zoochosis in the first place.

40 By writing out the first order and rewriting the order after each swap made by the owner of the car yard, you can focus on one change at a time. From the table below you can see that after the third day the Mercedes and Bentley are back where they started:

Left	←			→	Right
Start	Mercedes	Bentley	BMW	Toyota	Holden
Day 1	Holden	Toyota	BMW	Bentley	Mercedes
Day 2	Toyota	Holden	Bentley	BMW	Mercedes
Day 3	Mercedes	Bentley	Holden	BMW	Toyota

THINKING SKILLS Test 3

Page 47

1 D 2 C 3 B 4 D 5 B 6 C 7 A 8 D 9 B
10 D 11 C 12 A 13 C 14 A 15 A 16 B
17 D 18 B 19 C 20 C 21 D 22 A 23 D
24 D 25 B 26 A 27 B 28 C 29 B 30 D
31 C 32 B 33 A 34 A 35 A 36 D 37 D
38 B 39 D 40 A

1   The view from the back left of the solid is represented by A. B is the view from directly above or below the solid. C is the view from the front left of the solid. D is not the view from any side.

2   The argument is that dogs should be banned from the walkway because they are a threat to the Little Penguin colony. So you need to find the statement that **most** shows dogs are a threat. C is correct because causing the penguins to abandon their nests is an example of the kind of high-risk threat that dogs pose.

3   Any time you remove some of a solid, the volume decreases. This means you can rule out C and D. What happens to the surface area of the solid depends on the width, depth, height and shape of the amount removed. It is not necessary to find the surface area of the original shape. In this case, the original solid loses two square units from its surface area, the one on top and the one at the bottom where the hole emerges. However, looking inside the hole that's been created, you can see that 12 extra squares have been exposed. $12 - 2 = 10$. So the new solid has 10 more squares showing than the original solid. The surface area has increased. Therefore the solution is B.

4   Options A, B and C all use at least one tile that is a reflection of this tile. Tiles cannot be reflected, only rotated.

5   The text seems to want you to accept that the world's natural heritage is vulnerable to threats and that brave park rangers face life-threatening dangers defending it. The rest of the text gives you reasons to believe this main idea. It talks about the kinds of threats faced by the world's natural heritage and the dangers rangers face protecting it.

6   To find out what the scores were for task 4 you need to find out what the total score could have been. Mia currently has the highest combined score. Her minimum score is the total of her first three tasks, as this will be her total if she scores 0 (or anything below 6) on her last task. She cannot get less than 22: $10 + 7 + 5 = 22$. Seth's highest possible score would include his two scores of 6 and a perfect 10 in the last task. He cannot get more than 22: $6 + 6 + 10 = 22$. Therefore the

score must have been 22 as it is the only score that both Mia and Seth can get. For Kiara to get 22 she must have scored a 9 in her final task, to be added to the 8 and 5 she got in task 2 and task 3: $22 - 8 - 5 = 9$.

7   Kiara's fourth-highest score was 2. Seth's fourth-highest score was 3. Mia's fourth-highest score must have been below 5, otherwise she would have drawn with Nick. Nick's fourth score was 5, which is higher than the other students' fourth-highest score.

8   If whoever broke the window must have brought a ball **and** been in the playground before school, it follows that anyone who does not meet both these conditions cannot have broken the window. So if Arlo did not bring a ball to school, he cannot have broken the window.

9   First ask yourself what Blake's conclusion is. (Ruby loves mowing the lawn.) Next ask yourself what evidence he has based this conclusion on. (Ruby is mowing the lawn.) Finally read and think about each assumption listed. Blake has made the mistake of assuming that everyone who mows the lawn loves mowing the lawn. (Ruby is mowing the lawn + everyone who mows lawns loves mowing lawns = therefore Ruby loves mowing the lawn.)

10 If Sydney is 2 hours ahead of Perth, the first two clocks must be Sydney and Perth respectively, as no other clocks show a difference of 2 hours. If Toronto is 5 hours behind London, then London and Toronto must be the third and fifth clocks respectively, as the difference is 5 hours and London is ahead of Toronto. This means the fourth clock is Sao Paulo. It must be 8 am or 8 pm. As all time zones are within 24 hours of each other and Sydney is ahead of Sao Paulo, it cannot be 8 am, as this would mean Sao Paulo was a full 25 hours behind Sydney. So, as it is 9 am Tuesday in Sydney, it must be 7 am Tuesday in Perth. London is behind Perth so it must be 12 midnight. It must be 8 pm Monday in Sao Paulo and 7 pm Monday in Toronto. The wall should look like this:

Sydney | Perth | London | Sao Paulo | Toronto

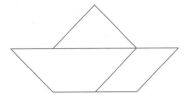

11 It is possible for all others by moving the grey circle.

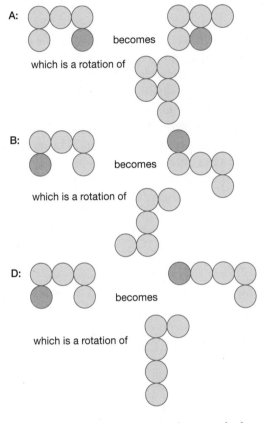

A:

[circles] becomes [circles]

which is a rotation of

B:

[circles] becomes [circles]

which is a rotation of

D:

[circles] becomes [circles]

which is a rotation of

It is impossible to move only one circle to create C.

12 The solutions for B, C and D are shown below:

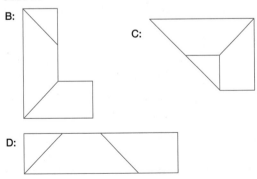

B:

C:

D:

For **A**, once the largest piece is placed, the spaces left over are not the same as the other two shapes:

13 Since David was an experienced cook, he only had to pass the audition. So if he was not chosen to be a contestant, he must have failed the audition.

14 The upgrade deal was for one extra item (cheese, a patty or chips) but Carlos ordered two extra items (cheese and chips).

15 Faisal argues that we should not use products containing palm oil because palm-oil plantations are harming the environment and wildlife. So you need to find the statement that **most** shows palm-oil plantations are harming the environment and wildlife. Habitat loss for endangered species is an example of harm to the environment and wildlife.

16 The coloured shapes are placed from the bottom up in the order black, blue, grey, white, with the white always on top. The next colour down is always grey. The colours are cycling through the shapes. Grey started in the ellipse, then went to the square, then to the triangle and will be in the circle for the fourth step of the pattern.

17 Nina's uncle's argument is that climbing Mount Everest will not be risky because he will have a Sherpa guide. The fact that there can be unpredictable icefalls and avalanches weakens the argument that having a Sherpa guide means there is no risk. (C might weaken the argument that the climb will be easy. This could mean there is some risk but it is not the statement that **most** weakens the argument about risk.)

18 The information tells us that anyone who is not creative cannot be a successful actor. Mo says he **might** not be creative but this does not mean he is **definitely** not creative. So his reasoning that **maybe** he won't be successful is correct. Aida says she will definitely be a successful actor and she appears to have the skills needed. However, the information does not say that someone with those skills will **definitely** be a successful actor. Aida's reasoning is therefore flawed.

19 Consider one team. It plays 3 teams 5 times each: 3 × 5 = 15 rounds. Four teams play 15 games each: 4 × 15 = 60 games. However, this counts each game twice as Central v South is the same as South v Central. 60 ÷ 2 = 30 round games. 30 + 2 finals games = 32 games.

20 The text seems to want you to accept the opening sentence: that balloons kill wildlife. You can check this by seeing whether the rest of the text gives you reasons to believe this main idea. In this case, the rest of the text provides examples of ways balloons can kill wildlife. This confirms the main idea and C is the statement that best expresses it.

21 From the information you can draw the conclusion that if Gia sleeps in, she will be late and if she is late, she has no chance of getting a place on the team.

22 The best way to answer this question is to pick an example. Choose a fraction less than one. In this case, you may choose one-half $(\frac{1}{2})$. Add the same number to the numerator and denominator to see the resulting fraction. In this case, you may add 2. $\frac{1+2}{2+2} = \frac{3}{4}$. Three-quarters is closer to one than one-half. No matter what fraction you choose, it will always be the case that the new fraction will be closer to one.

23 Marina's reasoning is incorrect because the information states that dogs with longer snouts are **generally** better at scent detection. This does not mean they **must** be better. Eric's reasoning is incorrect because the information states that dogs with short or flat faces are generally not as good at scent detection, not that they cannot smell anything.

24 If you are to use one of each coin, it is best to count these six coins straight away and work out what amount you have left: $2 + $1 + $0.50 + $0.20 + $0.10 + $0.05 = $3.85. Now you need to minimise the number of coins you use to make up the rest of the $14.50. $14.50 − $3.85 = $10.65. To make $10.65 with the minimum number of coins, you must use as many $2 coins as you can, followed by $1 coins, then 50c coins, and so on: 5 × $2 + 1 × $0.50 + 1 × $0.10 + 1 × $0.05 = $10.65. So you use 8 more coins. With the 6 coins you had to use, you need 14 coins altogether.

25 The third piece of information tells us the second and fifth columns represent rollerbladers and those who would not use the park, as these are the only columns of the same height. The second piece of information tells us the first column must represent skateboarders and the third must represent scooter-riders. This must be true, as one column must be twice as high as the other. So either the first and third columns or the fourth and the fifth/second show this relationship. If the fourth column represents skateboarders, then one of either the second or fifth columns must represent scooter-riders. This cannot be the case as those columns are already known to be representing rollerbladers and those who will not use the park at all. This means the fourth column represents bike riders. If the first column represents six people, then each mark on the vertical axis represents one person, so the fourth column represents four people. The final graph would look like this, though the 'rollerblades' and 'no use' columns could be switched.

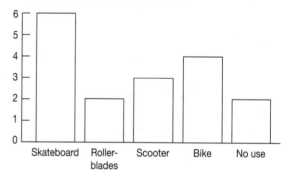

26 First ask yourself what Ella's conclusion is. (It is bin night so they need to put their bins out.) Next ask yourself what evidence she has based this conclusion on. (The neighbour has put his bins out.) For Ella's conclusion to hold, it must be assumed that people only put out their bins on bin night. (The neighbour's bin is out + people only put out their bins on bin night = therefore it is bin night.)

27 The largest frame cannot be on the far right as the third-largest frame is there. It cannot be on the far left as the smallest frame must always be to the left of it. So the largest frame must be in any one of the middle three spaces. If the second largest frame cannot be next to the largest then it can never be in the centre spot as the largest frame would then be next to it.

28 If Elliot likes two sports only, there are three possible combinations: canoeing and rowing, canoeing and archery, and rowing and archery. But you know that everyone who enjoys canoeing also likes rowing so Elliot cannot like canoeing and archery only. He must like canoeing and rowing or rowing and archery. In either case he likes rowing. You can see from this reasoning that A is incorrect as Elliot can like two sports, canoeing and rowing, without liking archery. B is incorrect as Elliot may like archery only. D is incorrect as you know some viewers liked watching all three sports.

29 If the temperature was over 25 degrees, they would have gone to the pool so it must be under 25 degrees. It is easy to think the answer must be A: that it rained. However, the group could have played a board game whether it rained or not, as it works with both Connor's and Grace's statements.

30 To be a successful musician you must be talented and lucky. This means you must be **both** talented and lucky. Layla is not talented; therefore she cannot be a successful musician.

31 Doug finished behind Rusty and Pongo was faster than Fido but not as fast as Doug. Beethoven was slower than Fido. So the race order must have been: Rusty, Doug, Pongo, Fido and then Beethoven. If third and fourth scored the same for behaviour, then Pongo and Fido scored the same. Beethoven scored higher than Pongo and Fido scored higher than Rusty. Therefore Beethoven must have scored higher than Rusty and they cannot have scored the same.

32 Tim is arguing that we need to save whales before it's too late. So you need to find the statement that **most** shows the need to save whales is urgent. The fact that there are so few whales left shows that soon it will be too late. (C would strengthen the argument that whales need to be saved but it is not the statement that **most** strengthens the argument that the need to save whales is urgent.)

33 From the information, the towns are set up as in the diagram below:

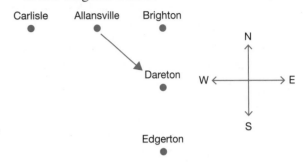

Dareton is south-east of Allansville.

34 It always helps to draw the scenario. You can then see that if John is diagonally opposite Percy, then for Kamal to be opposite Angela they must be at the ends of the table. Once you place Jim between Kamal and Percy, you can place Nick and John on the other side of the table. The diagram below shows the answer. The reflection of this is also possible and would give the same answer.

35 The information tells us everyone who would like a film club would also like a drama club and, since they like drama, they would also like a comedy club but not a coding club. So it is reasonable to draw the conclusion that if Ying would like a film club, she would not like a coding club.

36 For A, if Markus is from France then Paulo must be from England as he speaks English and French but is not the person from France. Similarly, Jan must be from Italy as he speaks English and Italian but is not from England. So A is true and is therefore incorrect.

For B, if Paulo is from England then Jan must be from Italy for the same reason as above. Laura speaks German and Italian but is not from Italy so she must be from Germany. So B is true and is therefore incorrect.

For C, if Markus is from Germany then Laura must be from Italy as she speaks German and Italian but is not from Germany. Jan must then be from England as he speaks Italian and English but is not from Italy. Paulo must be from France as he speaks English and French but is not from England. So C is true and is therefore incorrect.

For D, if Paulo is from France, it is possible that Jan is from Italy (if Markus is from England and Laura is from Germany) but it is also possible that Jan is from England (if Markus is from Germany and Laura is from Italy). Therefore this is not necessarily true. D is the correct answer.

37 There can be clouds without rain so A is incorrect. There can be clouds without rain so B is incorrect. C is therefore also incorrect.

38 Even though someone who did not compete last month will be selected this month, it does not follow that someone who competed last month will not be selected this month. So Levi may still be selected to compete.

39 Alice's reasoning is incorrect because, even though the information tells us that whenever Finn leaves his toy elephant at daycare he always cries, it does not follow that this is the only thing that makes Finn cry. So he might still cry on the way home. Fran's reasoning is not correct for the same reason. Something else might have made Finn cry.

40 While the company is hoping people will think the answer is D, the claim does not actually say this. If 9 out of 10 men kept **or** regrew their hair, the other man must have lost his hair. Of those 9 men, it might be that none regrew any hair and they just kept the hair they already had. So the product might do absolutely nothing. While B, C and D might all be true, the company's claim does not support them. The product might work but only for some people, as you know it doesn't work for the 1 man in 10 who lost his hair.

THINKING SKILLS Test 4   Page 57

1 B 2 C 3 B 4 A 5 C 6 B 7 A 8 D 9 B
10 A 11 D 12 B 13 C 14 A 15 C 16 C
17 A 18 D 19 B 20 B 21 B 22 D 23 A
24 A 25 D 26 D 27 D 28 D 29 B 30 C
31 A 32 C 33 B 34 D 35 D 36 C 37 C
38 B 39 A 40 A

1 The clock strikes once at 1 am, twice at 2 am and all the way to 12 times at 12 noon.

$$1 + 2 + 3 + 4 + 5 + 6 + 7 + 8 + 9 + 10 + 11 + 12$$
$$= (1+12)+(2+11)+(3+10)+(4+9)+(5+8)+(6+7)$$
$$= 6 \times 13$$
$$= 78$$

The clock will strike another 78 times between 12 noon and 12 midnight.

Total strikes $= 78 + 78$
                $= 156$

The cuckoo springs through its doors twice for each strike. $156 \times 2 = 312$. The cuckoo springs through the door 312 times each day.

2 First ask yourself what Joe's conclusion is. (Chocolate sponge is Evie's favourite cake.) Next ask yourself what evidence he has based this conclusion on. (Evie's dad made it for her birthday.) For Joe's conclusion to hold, it must be assumed that everyone gets their favourite cake on their birthday. (Evie's dad made chocolate sponge cake for Evie's birthday + everyone gets their favourite cake on their birthday = therefore chocolate sponge is Evie's favourite cake.)

3 If the three numbers multiply to 24, there are 6 options.

$1 \times 1 \times 24$	sum $= 1 + 1 + 24 = 26$
$1 \times 2 \times 12$	sum $= 1 + 2 + 12 = 15$
$1 \times 3 \times 8$	sum $= 1 + 3 + 8 = 12$
$1 \times 4 \times 6$	sum $= 1 + 4 + 6 = 11$
$2 \times 2 \times 6$	sum $= 2 + 2 + 6 = 10$
$2 \times 3 \times 4$	sum $= 2 + 3 + 4 = 9$

Only the last option satisfies Callan's comment that the sum of his siblings' scores beat his, even though he was the top scorer. He scored 4 goals. His brother and sister scored 2 and 3. Therefore the family has 9 pets.

4 The passenger starts to fall asleep when the bus has travelled one-quarter of the distance and continues sleeping until the halfway point. The passenger then falls asleep for three-quarters of the remaining distance, which is three-quarters of half the trip. This is three-eighths. So the total sleeping time is one-quarter plus three-eighths, which is five-eighths. The portion of time asleep is shown by the coloured sections below:

Start   Finish

5 From the information you can draw the conclusion that if Dora's parents are unhappy with her, there is no way they will let her go to the party. So this conclusion cannot be true.

6

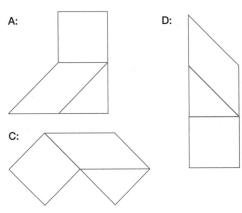

A:

D:

C:

For B, the only place the square can go is in the middle, as shown below. This leaves three triangular spaces to fill with only two pieces.

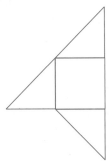

7 Working back from Stop D we can note that one-third of the passengers got off the bus, leaving 10 passengers remaining. So 10 must be two-thirds of the number of passengers who arrived at Stop D. That means 5 is one-third so 5 got off the bus. The bus must have arrived at Stop D with 15 passengers: $10 \div 2 \times 3 = 15$. Now, 15 passengers left Stop C. When the bus arrived at Stop C, half the passengers got off, then 2 got on. So, when following the bus in reverse, we take away the 2 passengers and double the number left to get the number of passengers who arrived at Stop C.

$(15 - 2) \times 2 = 13 \times 2$
$= 26$

So 26 passengers arrived at Stop C. When the bus arrived at Stop B, 3 passengers got off and 8 got on. So, when following the bus in reverse, we take away the 8 and add the 3.

This will give us the number of passengers on the bus when it arrived at Stop B, which is the same number as when the bus departed from Stop A: $26 - 8 + 3 = 21$. The bus departed from Stop A with 21 passengers.

Another way of answering this question would be to follow the steps the right way starting with each of the options.

8 The text seems to want you to accept the opening sentence: that it is feasible to refill an electric vehicle's battery for free. You can check this by seeing whether the rest of the text gives you reasons to believe this main idea. In this case, the rest of the text provides examples of ways to recharge an EV for free. This confirms the main idea and D is the statement that best expresses it.

9 The information tells us police officer was less popular than firefighter, which in turn was less popular than author and wildlife carer. Football player must fill the spot between author and firefighter since firefighter was three behind wildlife carer. So it follows that police officer was the least popular choice.

10 Jun must have enough tiles to make eight copies of his pattern. In A, there are two of the tiles with triangles on them. $2 \times 8 = 16$. This means Jun needs 16 of these tiles in the final design. He only has 15 of those tiles left so he cannot use this design. He can make B, C and D, as he has enough of each of the tiles.

11 Jack's parents' argument is that children should not use social media because it is dangerous and distracting. D provides a positive outcome for children using social media and so weakens their argument.

12 If Samim splits the hens evenly after the first night, in the morning there will be two eggs in one section of the chook pen and two eggs in the other. One section will have a white egg and a brown egg:

He knows the two hens in the section with two white eggs lay white only. He can then put one of the chickens from the other part of the chook pen in with them for the second night. If that section has two white and one brown the following day, the hen he moved is laying the brown egg.

If that section has three white eggs, then there will be a brown egg in the section with only one hen in it. Either way, he will know which hen is laying the brown egg.

13 Any time we remove some of a solid, the volume decreases. This means we can rule out A and D. What happens to the surface area of the solid depends on the width, depth, height and shape of the amount removed. It is not necessary to find the surface area of the original shape. In this case, the original solid loses 8 square units from its surface: one from the top, one from the bottom and three down each side that makes up the original edge. Six new square units are exposed after the transformation. If we lose 8 and gain 6, we have essentially lost two. So the new solid has lost 2 square units from its surface area. The volume and the surface area have decreased. Therefore the answer is C.

14 Since Mr Lin is both a member and on the mailing list, he would have needed to apply online to get the free tickets.

15 Both Yitong's and Ben's reasoning is correct. Yitong is correct because if their tallies for fiction were different but their tallies for nonfiction were the same, the overall number of books read could not be equal. Ben is correct because if their tallies for nonfiction were the same but their tallies for fiction were different, the overall number of books read could not be equal.

16 Knowing Lincoln is in 16 and Amy lives across the street in 133, you can work out how many houses are in the street. There are 15 houses before Lincoln's on his side of the street so there must be 15 houses past Amy's on her side of the street—but counting up: 133 + 15 = 148. There are 148 houses in the street, with numbers 1 to 74 up one side and 75 to 148 down the other side. Note that the numbers of houses directly opposite each will always add up to 149. For example, 1 + 148 = 149, 2 + 147 = 149, etc.—all the way up to 74 + 75 = 149. 149 – 100 = 49. So Miles lives in number 49.

17 This statement gives further evidence to support the argument that it was birds' intelligence that helped them to survive the dinosaur extinction.

18 Even though anyone who did not get a chance to help in the kitchen last term will get a chance this term, it does not follow that anyone who did help last term will not get a chance this term. So Anya may still get a chance.

19 When solving questions of this type, it helps to insert spaces in the sequence for the missing dates. Then use arrows to see what each combination will cover. For example, we can see that two weekly passes will not cover all dates so A ($500) is not possible:

| 4 | 5 | 6 | | | 9 | 10 | 11 | 12 | | 14 | | | 17 | 18 |

The best combination is:

| 4 | 5 | 6 | | | 9 | 10 | 11 | 12 | | 14 | | | 17 | 18 |

A 3-day pass for 4, 5 and 6 August	$140
A weekly pass for 9–15 August	$250
Two daily passes for 17 and 18 August	$120
Total	$510

20 The information states that anyone interested in karate was also interested in lacrosse and, since they were interested in lacrosse, they were not interested in fencing. So it is reasonable to draw the conclusion that if Jade is interested in karate, she does not want fencing.

21 First ask yourself what Max's conclusion is. (Bree must know a lot about climate change.) Next ask yourself what evidence he has based this conclusion on. (Bree is about to prepare a speech on climate change.) For Max's conclusion to hold, it must be assumed that students only give speeches about topics they know a lot about. (Bree is about to prepare a speech on climate change + students only give speeches about topics they know a lot about = therefore Bree must know a lot about climate change.)

22 If the Festival runs for exactly 21 days, this is three weeks: $21 \div 7 = 3$. It does not matter which day the festival starts on. Whichever day the festival starts on, there will be three of each of the days of the week. Two performances on three days of the week: $2 \times 3 = 6$. Three performances on two days of the week: $3 \times 2 = 6$. So in seven days she will perform 12 times: $6 + 6 = 12$. In 21 days she will perform 36 times: $12 \times 3 = 36$.

23 The argument is that in a battle between a great white shark and a saltwater crocodile, the shark would win. A most strengthens that argument. Cameron says the shark is 'wider than the crocodile's mouth' so the crocodile won't be able to fit the shark in its mouth and therefore won't cause maximum damage.

24 This question requires us to estimate the amount of space each sector (piece of pie) takes up. There are many ways to do this. One way to approach a question like this is to eliminate any answers that must be wrong to see what you are left with. To do this we can compare the ratios of one section to the other sections to see if the graph makes sense. The largest sector is a little less than half of the chart. The other two sectors add to more than

half. The two smallest amounts (14 and 21) add to 35 so their two sectors cannot together be more than either 39 or 46. So the missing colour cannot be bay or chestnut. Bay is the largest sector shown and chestnut is the second largest. The remaining sector is about one-third that of chestnut so it must be dappled grey. The missing amount must be black.

25 The second (or middle) component of the object must look like a square from above. The second component in this option could be a square only if we are looking directly at one of its sides, as there is no mark to signify we are looking at one of the corners/edges. There are marks on the same component in B and C, showing us that the width of the component is the diagonal of the square rather than the side. Therefore, when looking from above, this second component would completely block out our ability to see the sphere underneath it.

26 You can draw the conclusion that the order of preference was: comedy, fantasy, adventure, science-fiction. All we know about musicals is they were preferred over adventure or science-fiction. We do not have enough information to rank musicals further. Musicals could have tied with fantasy, been more popular than fantasy, tied with comedy or been more popular than comedy. Therefore the statement that musicals could not have been the most preferred genre cannot be true.

27 There are two vehicles between the green car and the second white car so, if the first car is white, the green car and second white car must be second and fifth in some order. If the green car is second and the white car fifth, there is no place for the red car directly behind a white car so the second white car must be second and the green car fifth. This means the red car will be third. The remaining place will be for the truck. So the truck is the fourth vehicle.

28 Those who like chocolate are split into those who also like strawberry, those who like strawberry and vanilla, and those who only like chocolate. As more people like pistachio than just chocolate and all those who like pistachio like strawberry but not chocolate, more people like strawberry than chocolate.

All those who like pistachio or vanilla also like strawberry. So more people must like strawberry than any other flavour. A is incorrect for the reasons stated above. B is possibly true but it is not clear from the information given. It is not the solution that **must** be true. C is possibly true but we have no evidence to support this. It is not the solution that **must** be true.

29 The question tells you the bushwalkers stuck to their deals. Camelia is implying she would **only** cook dinner if Oscar set up the tents so we know that Oscar **must** have set up the tents. As Petra said she would build the fire if Oscar set up the tents, we know Petra **must** have set up the tents. However, while Oscar said he'd set up the tents if they walked over 10 km, he didn't say this was the **only** reason he'd set up the tents so we don't know that they definitely walked over 10 km.

30 If she practised her scales and her performance piece every day, she would have passed her exam. She did not pass so she cannot have practised both every day.

31 It is best to approach this question by looking at booking slots for the house in a table. There are three family slots each for four weeks:

	Family 1	Family 2	Family 3
Week 1			
Week 2			
Week 3			
Week 4			

We know the Jones and Sullivan families must be separated, and the Jones family books in for weeks 1 and 2 in the Family 1 column. We can then book the Sullivans in for weeks 3 and 4 in the Family 1 column.

The Khan family wants to spend time with both the Jones and Sullivan families, and we know they holiday for two consecutive weeks so they can be booked in for weeks 2 and 3 in the Family 2 column.

Every family except the Muscat family must be booked in for two consecutive weeks so we know the Family 3 column will have the Edgecombe and Brady families. That means the Muscat family will be Family 2 in weeks 1 and 4.

	Family 1	Family 2	Family 3
Week 1	Jones	Muscat	Edgecombe/ Brady
Week 2	Jones	Khan	Edgecombe/ Brady
Week 3	Sullivan	Khan	Brady/ Edgecombe
Week 4	Sullivan	Muscat	Brady/ Edgecombe

If the Edgecombe family is booked in for weeks 1 and 2, then the Brady family will not be holidaying with the Jones or the Edgecombe families. If the Edgecombe family is booked in for weeks 3 and 4, the Brady family will not holiday with the Sullivan or Edgecombe family.

Whatever the case, they will not be holidaying with the Edgecombe family.

32 The text seems to want you to accept that Indigenous rangers do important work caring for country. The rest of the text provides examples of work the rangers do caring for country, with the final sentence mentioning how important this work is. So that confirms C as the main idea.

33 The most important information in this question is the fact that **none of the barrels are now labelled correctly**. This means there are only two possible arrangements for the labels. These are shown in the table below:

	Apple Barrel	Orange Barrel	Mixed Barrel
Labels	MIXED	APPLE	ORANGE
Labels	ORANGE	MIXED	APPLE

There is no way to tell which label goes where unless you pick a piece of fruit from the barrel, so we can rule out A. By picking a piece of fruit from the barrel labelled MIXED, we can relabel the barrels. If we pick out an apple, we know this is the apple barrel as it cannot be the orange barrel and as it is labelled MIXED it cannot be the mixed barrel. The barrel labelled APPLE must be the orange barrel and the barrel labelled ORANGE must be mixed. The same process can be used if the fruit is an orange.

If we pick a piece of fruit from one of the barrels labelled APPLE or ORANGE we cannot with certainty say which barrel it has come from.

34 If the rooster crows, it must be after sunrise. However, this does not rule out the possibility that today the rooster didn't crow at all. It could be before or after sunrise but Mr and Mrs Reyes are both wrong to draw conclusions based on the rooster not crowing.

35 Neither Kinta's nor Ava's reasoning is correct. No information is given about the meaning of a filter light that is on continuously. So Kinta's reasoning that the filter **must** be blocked has a flaw. The information states that a flashing yellow light always means the filter needs cleaning but this does not rule out that the filter might need cleaning without the light flashing; it might be broken, for example. So Ava's reasoning is flawed.

36 As Karel's motor skills are excellent for his age, all he has to do to get accepted is to pass the standing jump test. He did not get accepted, so he must not have passed the standing jump test. While it is clear that he therefore must not have done well in the standing jump test, this is not the reason he did not get accepted. It was not necessary for Karel to do well in the standing jump test; all he had to do was pass. Therefore B is not the reason he did not get accepted.

37 If West Coast won and GWS lost, then West Coast would be in the top eight. As GWS and Essendon are the teams in the top eight, this cannot be true. For A, if GWS and Essendon both lose, they can still make the top eight if the other two teams lose. For B, if West Coast and Fremantle win, GWS and Essendon can still make the top eight by winning their own games.

38 The argument is that handfeeding dolphins is a harmful practice. The fact that handfeeding negatively impacts the whole ecosystem adds to the list of harmful consequences given by the marine biologist. Therefore it most strengthens the argument.

39 Sophie has not thought that any gardener who entered for ten years might also have come first, second or third and therefore would receive two ribbons. Five ribbons will be awarded but they may not go to five gardeners.

40 From the information in the box it is clear that Colin is looking at a male crocodile, as any egg incubated at 31.7 degrees will produce a male. Any temperature above or below will **most likely** produce a female but might also produce a male. So options B, C and D are all possible.

MATHEMATICAL REASONING Test 1 Page 68

1 A 2 C 3 A 4 C 5 B 6 A 7 D 8 D 9 E
10 B 11 D 12 D 13 C 14 E 15 C 16 C
17 B 18 E 19 C 20 D 21 E 22 E 23 B
24 B 25 B 26 D 27 E 28 B 29 A 30 A
31 C 32 A 33 E 34 E 35 C

1 In this problem you have to remember to do the multiplications first then the additions. So $2 \times 8 = 16$ and $7 \times 6 = 42$, then $16 + 9 + 42 = 67$.

2 Three times 40 is 120 plus half of 40 is 20, making 140 km.

3 Do this problem in two steps. First find three and a quarter hours before 9.30 pm which is 6.15 pm and then convert this to 24-hour time, namely 1815. Another way to solve this problem is to convert 9.30 pm to 24-hour time, which is 2130, and then subtract 315 which leaves you with 1815.

4 There is only one chance in four of getting two heads. All the possible alternatives of getting heads (H) and tails (T) are:

HH   HT   TT   TH

5 One-quarter of a kilogram is 250 g, so one-quarter of $8 is $2.00.

6 Here is another step-by-step problem. It has two parts. First work out the distance it travels at 80 km per hour, which is $3\frac{1}{2} \times 80 = 280$ km. Next work out how far it travels at 70 km per hour and this is 140 km. The last step is to add the 280 and the 140 to give you 420 km. Some students race through this and make simple errors. Remember: step by step.

7 This is a harder problem. You will need to do some thinking to solve this. Let's look at what you already know: first, the total number of 50c and 10c sweets equals 24. This is really important. Second, if you multiply the number of sweets by their price they should add up to $8.

You can solve this using an equation but you probably haven't been shown this way. Instead, you could work from the options. So let's look at each option and work backwards. The options show the number of 50-cent sweets, so we can easily work out the number of 10-cent sweets because they must total 24. Then we multiply each sweet by its price. Here are the five options.

	50c	Total	10c	Total	50c + 10c
A	10	$5	14	$1.40	$6.40
B	12	$6	12	$1.20	$7.20
C	16	$8	8	$0.80	$8.80
D	14	$7	10	$1.00	$8.00
E	18	$9	6	$0.60	$9.60

The customer bought 14 50-cent sweets and 10 10-cent sweets.

8 The area of the total square is 4 square units so deduct the area of the unshaded part of 1 square unit from that to get the area of the shaded part of 3 square units.

9 The train travels at 200 km per hour. This means it would take 2 hours to travel 400 km.

10 One truck is equal to the weight of two sedans, so a sedan is half the weight of a truck.

11 The opposite sides of the dice are 6, 5, 4 and 3, which give a total of 18.

12 The two numbers are 998 and 12 and Bruce multiplies them. Consider 998 as 2 less than 1000. As $1000 \times 12 - 2 \times 12 = 12\,000 - 24 = 11\,976$, Bruce's result is 11 976.

13 The question is to find the fraction of the circle that is shaded. There are 360° in a revolution. As $360 - 240 = 120$ and $\frac{120}{360} = \frac{1}{3}$, one-third of the circle is shaded. As $480 \div 3 = 160$, the area shaded is 160 cm².

14 Look for numbers 1 less than a multiple of 4 **and** 6. Here are multiples of 12: 12, 24, 36, 48, 60 … The smallest number larger than 40 is $48 - 1 = 47$.

15 Out of the 20 squares, 8 are unshaded. As $\frac{1}{5}$ of 20 is $20 \div 5 = 4$, and $8 - 4 = 4$, there needs to be 4 more squares shaded.

16 There are many answers but remember Pablo is older than 21. As $(43 - 1)$ is a multiple of 6 and $(43 + 2)$ is a multiple of 5, then Pablo is 43 years old.

17 A line of symmetry cuts the shape in half. There are 4 lines of symmetry.

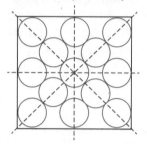

18 Look at the net to work out opposite faces. 4 and 6 are on opposite faces and $4 \times 6 = 24$. 12 is on the opposite face to *. As $* \times 12 = 24$, then $* = 2$.

19 First, work out the number of balls that are repeating. As $1 + 2 + 1 + 3 + 1 = 8$, there are 8 balls repeating. As $36 \div 8 = 4$, and remainder 4, the 36th ball is the same as the 4th ball, which is green.

20 Look for a complete row, column or diagonal to work out the magic number. As $12 + 10 + 9 + 15 = 46$, every row, column or diagonal has a sum of 46. The number replacing the * is 8.

19	5	6	16
8	14	13	11
12	10	9	15
7	17	18	4

21 Work out the rule for the sequence. As the sequence is $1^2 = 1$, $2^2 = 4$, $3^2 = 9$, $4^2 = 16$, and so on, the numbers are the square numbers larger than 0. A feature of the list is the difference between the squares can be calculated by using the sum of consecutive terms. The difference between the ninth and tenth terms is 19 and 9 + 10 = 19. As $9^2 = 81$ and $10^2 = 100$, then 100 + 81 = 181.

22 Add the fractions together and subtract from 1 to find the remaining fraction.

$1 - (\frac{1}{3} + \frac{1}{4} + \frac{1}{5})$

$= 1 - (\frac{20}{60} + \frac{15}{60} + \frac{12}{60})$

$= \frac{60}{60} - \frac{47}{60} = \frac{13}{60}$

23 When finding a percentage of a quantity you can change the percentage to a fraction. Here 10% is one-tenth, and so divide the quantity by 10. 10% of 40 is 40 ÷ 10 = 4. As (40 − 4) ÷ 2 = 18, and 18 − 4 = 14, Nicola has 14 apples remaining.

24 To find the missing number, simplify the number sentence by using the rules for order of operations. As 80 ÷ $\boxed{?}$ − (2 + 6) × 4 = 8 then 80 ÷ $\boxed{?}$ − 8 × 4 = 8. This means 80 ÷ $\boxed{?}$ − 32 = 8, and so 80 ÷ $\boxed{?}$ = 40. The missing number is 2.

25 As the shapes are squares, there is already a horizontal line of symmetry. Ronan needs to add 4 more tiles to have a vertical line of symmetry.

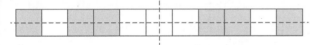

26 An equilateral triangle has 3 equal sides, and an isosceles triangle has 2 equal sides. As 4 × 3 = 12, the equilateral triangle has a perimeter of 12 cm. As 12 × 2 = 24, the isosceles triangle has a perimeter of 24 cm. The triangle can have dimensions 9 cm, 9 cm and 6 cm.

27 As product means to multiply and quotient means to divide, the number sentence is 2(4 + 2 × 6) > 18 − 8 ÷ 4.

28 As 168 ÷ 8 = 21, the tower has 21 cubes. Counting the cubes in each of the towers, the pattern is 1, 3, 6, 10 … This is a pattern of triangular numbers. The list is 1, 3, 6, 10, 15, 21 … As the sixth term is 21, the sixth tower is 6 cubes high. As each cube has a side length of 2 cm, the height is 12 cm.

29 As $1 - \frac{1}{4} = \frac{3}{4}$, one-quarter empty means three-quarters full. The container has 84 L when three-quarters full. When the container is three-quarters empty, it is one-quarter full. As 84 ÷ 3 = 28, the container has 28 L when one-quarter full.

30 Different places in the world have different local times. This means there are time differences between cities across the world. 2220 to 2400 is 1 h 40 minutes, plus 19 h 05 min is 20 h 45 min.

As Dubai is 8 hours ahead of New York, subtract 8 h to get the flight time of 12 h 45 min.

31 Suppose the dimensions of rectangle I are 2 cm by 1 cm. The area of rectangle I is 2 cm². As 2 × 2 × 4 = 16, the dimensions of rectangle III are 16 cm by 1 cm. The area of rectangle III is 16 cm². As 16 ÷ 2 = 8, there are 8 rectangle Is that will cover rectangle III.

32 Each of the three statements need to be checked first. As 5 − 2 = 3, there were 3 more students who liked purple than yellow. Statement 1 is not correct. As 2 + 2 = 4 and 1 + 2 + 5 + 6 + 2 = 16, then a quarter of students liked green or yellow. Statement 2 is correct. As 1 + 2 = 3 and 3 × 2 = 6, then twice as many people liked red than the total of the students who like blue or green. Statement 3 is correct. Statements 2 and 3 are correct.

33

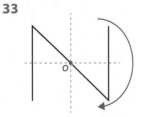

34 The shape is a rectangle minus 2 small rectangles. As 14 × 10 − 2 × 6 × 2 = 116, the area is 116 cm².

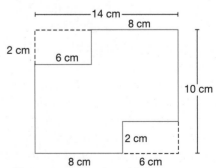

35 There are 360° in a revolution. As $\frac{90}{360} = \frac{1}{4}$, one-quarter of the cars were grey. As $60 \div 4 = 15$, there were 15 grey cars in the car park. Statement 1 is correct. As $120 + 60 = 180$ and half of 360 is 180, half of the cars were white or red. Statement 2 is correct. As $360 - (90 + 120 + 60) = 90$, and $\frac{90}{360} = \frac{1}{4}$, there should be 15 cars that are not white, grey or red. Statement 3 is not correct. Statements 1 and 2 are correct.

MATHEMATICAL REASONING Test 2

Page 73

1 D **2** B **3** C **4** E **5** A **6** A **7** C **8** B **9** B
10 A **11** C **12** A **13** D **14** B **15** C **16** A
17 A **18** D **19** D **20** E **21** C **22** B **23** C
24 E **25** E **26** D **27** C **28** B **29** C **30** A
31 E **32** B **33** D **34** E **35** B

1 The square root of 169 is 13. Get someone to test you on the squares of all numbers up to 25. $(13 \times 10) \div (5 \times 2)$ is $130 \div 10 = 13$.

2 $19.8 \div 4 = 4.95$, $22.4 \div 10 \times 3 = 2.24 \times 3 = 6.72$ and $13.7 \div 10 \times 4 = 1.37 \times 4 = 5.48$. As $4.95 + 6.72 + 5.48 = 17.15$, the total cost is $17.15.

3 The even numbers are I, III and V. For I, II, III and IV you do not need to calculate the entire sums—all you need is to look at the last digit. In the case of V, 96, 84 and 72 are all divisible by 12, and $72 \div 12 = 6$, which is even.

4 Sixty (60) is the only number they say together. Just in case you are not clear on this, here is the list.
12: 108 96 84 72 60 48 36 24 12 0
10: 110 100 90 80 70 60 50 40 30 20 10 0

5 Although shape D might look as though it is correct, it is shape A that folds into the prism. Remember to draw some feint lines on the test paper to help you visualise the shape of the prism.

6 The faces represent the familiar Roman numerals. I = ☹ ; V = 😐; X = 😊.

7 The daily sales are $100, $110, $121, $133.10 and $146.41.

8 This square is reversed, with the highest numbers on the left. Each row decreases by four while the columns increase by 12 then 14. There are very few clues to help you so you need to try a number of solutions.

10	6	2
22	18	14
36	32	28

9 List as many factors of each one as you can and then see which are in common. Take the highest common factor, which is 8.

10 The missing number is 14 squared or 196.

11 The figure closest to $50 million is $49 507 861.

12 The ✳ is a minus sign and the ❖ is a plus sign. In questions like this you can always try each of the four options to see which is correct.

13 The amount is made up of 7 h for $70 plus 1 h unpaid break plus 3 h for $45 giving a total of $115.

14 The total area of the rectangle is 12 square units and the shaded portion is 2 square units, leaving 10 square units in the unshaded portion.

15 Calculate how much each jar weighs (2600 divided by 10) as a first step then multiply this by six to give 1560g or 1.56 kg.

16 Work out the number of minutes the movie ran. From 8:50 to 10:30 is 1 h 40 min, which is 100 min. From 8:50 to 10:00 is 1 h 10 min, which is 70 min. Steve watched 70 min out of 100 min, which is $\frac{70}{100} = 70\%$.

17 When the ball bounces up a certain height, it falls the same distance. As $50 \div 5 \times 2 = 20$, the ball rises to 20 m after bounce 1.
As $20 \div 5 \times 2 = 8$, the ball rises to 8 m after bounce 2. The ball falls 50 m, rises and falls 20 m, then rises and falls 8 m.
As $50 + 2 \times 20 + 2 \times 8 = 50 + 40 + 16 = 106$, the ball has travelled 106 m.

18 The average monthly maximum temperature in August was 17°. Statement 1 is not correct. As $30 - 17 = 13$, the range in temperature was 13°. Statement 2 is correct. As $26 - 21 = 5$, the greatest rise was 5° in October. Statement 3 is correct. Statements 2 and 3 are correct.

19 Brooke needs to add 5 tiles.

B	G	R	R	B	G	R	G	B	R	R	G	B

20 The number of matches used for each pattern is summarised in the table:

Pattern	1	2	3
Matches	5	9	13

The rule is Matches = 4 × Pattern + 1.
As 4 × 20 + 1 = 81, Leigh will use 81 matches.

21 As 24 – 18 = 6 and 24 – 12 = 12, the shaded rectangle has side lengths 12 cm and 6 cm. As 12 × 6 = 72, the area is 72 cm².

22 As $\frac{5}{6}$ of 240 = 240 ÷ 6 × 5 = 200, each glass will have 200 mL of juice. As 2 L = 2000 mL, and 2000 ÷ 200 = 10, Sharni will use 10 glasses.

23 Probability is the chance of an event happening. Two out of every 5 balls are red which means there could be 2 out of 5, 4 out of 10, 6 out of 15 and so on. Look for a smallest common multiple of 5 and 4 to be the total number of balls in the bag. As 5 × 4 = 20, the fractions could be rewritten as $\frac{2}{5} = \frac{8}{20}$ and $\frac{1}{4} = \frac{5}{20}$. This means there could be 8 red balls, 5 blue balls and 20 – (8 + 5) = 7 green balls.

24 Distance is Speed × Time. As 75 × 2 = 150, the distance is 150 km. As 75 + 25 = 100, his new average speed would be 100 km/h. As Time = Distance ÷ Speed, and 150 ÷ 100 = 1.5, it would take 1 h 30 min. This means the trip would have been shorter by 30 min.

25 As 5.1 = 5.10, you need to find the average of 4.38 and 5.10.
As (4.38 + 5.10) ÷ 2 = 9.48 ÷ 2 = 4.74, the value of X is 4.74.

26 As $1 - \frac{1}{3} = \frac{2}{3}$, it will take twice as long to finish the job. As 1 h 35 min is 95 min, and 95 × 2 = 190, it will take 190 min, which is 3 h 10 min.

27 0840 Friday plus 11 h 50 min is 2030 Friday, Paris time. Subtract 9 h so the plane arrives in Los Angeles at 1130 Friday.

28 The space inside the 12 rectangles is also a square with side length 10 cm.
As 14 × 14 – 10 × 10 = 196 – 100 = 96, and 96 ÷ 12 = 8, the area of each rectangle is 8 cm².

29 There are 2 lines of symmetry.

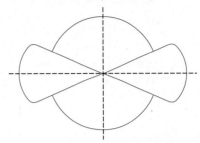

30 After her first spin, Dakota is facing west. After the second she is facing north-east.

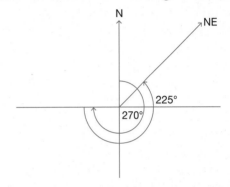

31 Suppose Frida's number is X. Multiplying by 6 and then dividing by 3 is like doubling. She has X + X + 4 – 2 – X + 5 – X which is 7.

32 As 600 + 540 + 620 = 1760, the mass of 2 mangos + 2 tomatoes + 2 apples is 1760 g. As 1760 ÷ 2 = 880, the total mass is 880 g.

33 As 40 + 70 + 80 + 75 + 105 = 370, the school raised $370.

34 As there are 60 minutes in an hour and 360° in a revolution then 1 minute = 6°, and half a minute is 3°. As 90 + 6 + 6 + 3 = 105, the angle is 105°.

35 There are 4 red balls out of 12. This is a probability of $\frac{1}{3}$. Statement 1 is not correct. There are 2 green balls and 1 yellow ball. This means a green ball is twice as likely to be chosen as a yellow ball. Statement 2 is correct. As 1 + 2 = 3 there are 3 balls that are either yellow or purple. There are 3 blue balls. Statement 3 is correct. Statements 2 and 3 are correct.

MATHEMATICAL REASONING Test 3   Page 78

1 C 2 A 3 E 4 D 5 D 6 B 7 A 8 D 9 C
10 B 11 A 12 A 13 D 14 A 15 B 16 B
17 C 18 D 19 D 20 E 21 C 22 C 23 B
24 B 25 A 26 C 27 A 28 D 29 E 30 A
31 C 32 E 33 B 34 C 35 E

1   There is a method for solving these types of problems using two equations at once. You will be shown this in high school. For the moment look at each of the four options and see if they fit the question. Take the first option of 8 as an example. In 2 years' time the son would be 10 (if you chose option A) and the father would be 30, whereas in 10 years' time the son's age would be 18 which would make the father 62 years (that is, 80 – 18 = 62). The first calculation of being 30 in 2 years' time and then being 62 in 10 years' time does not make sense, so this is clearly wrong. Try the correct option of 14. In 2 years the son will be 16 and the father 48 (3 × 16 = 48) whereas in 10 years' time the son will be 24 and the father should be 80 – 24 or 56 years old. This matches the first part of your calculations; that is, the father is now 46.

If you are having trouble, try to use the options as a guide. Also remember that most of these questions involve a number of steps.

2   Up to 3 pm the watch had lost 6 min per hour which means 36 min and add on 3 min lost during the half hour from 3 to 3.30 pm. This means that 39 min have to be subtracted from 3.30 pm, to give 2.51.

3   In 1210, 1 (in the tens column) is half of 2 (in the hundreds column).

4   This magic square uses all the numbers from 1 to 16. The total across, down and diagonally is 34. If you have trouble with this, try using one of the options as a start. It is advisable to complete the square just to check that you have not made a mistake. The completed square is:

16	3	2	13
5	10	11	8
9	6	7	12
4	15	14	1

5   Use the third hobbyist as the measure which is common to all. The first has three more than the third; the second has three times the number of the first which means that the second hobbyist has three times as many plus nine. Add all these together to get a first idea of the total number and you get five times the third hobbyist's number plus 12. Since the total is 27, then five times the number of birds must be equal to 15 which means that the third collector has three. If all these steps have been difficult to follow then get someone to explain it in a way that can help you. As a last resort you can use the five answers on a trial-and-error basis.

6   200 000 cents equals $2000, making the total $202 000.

7   The amount placed each day is: day 1, $1; day 2, $2; day 3, $4; day 4, $8; day 5, $16; day 6, $32; day 7, $64; day 8, $128; day 9, $256 each; day 10, $512; day 11, $1024; day 12, $2048; day 13, $4096; day 14, $8192 and day 15, $16 384.

8   The total runs scored over 10 innings was 450 and for 11 innings the total was 550, meaning that the eleventh innings required 100 runs to average 50.

9   The cumulative total of even numbers is: 2, then 6 (that is, 2 + 4), 12 (that is, 2 + 4 + 6), 20, 30, 42, 56, 72, 90, 110, 132, 156, 182, 210, 240, 272, and 306. There are 17 numbers.

10 Whenever two odd numbers are added together, the answer is always an even number.

11 In this case 90% is equal to $180, so 100% is equal to $200.

12 Consider the difference between each pair of numbers: 7 – 4 = 3, 16 – 7 = 9, 43 – 16 = 27, 124 – 43 = 81. Now write these differences as a sequence: 3, 9, 27, 81. The rule for these numbers is multiply by 3. As 81 × 3 = 243 and 124 + 243 = 367, the next number in the original sequence will be 367.

13 The answer must be an even number because it is like multiplying by two.

14 The passenger starts to fall asleep when the bus has travelled one-quarter of the distance and continues sleeping until the halfway point. The passenger then falls asleep for three-quarters of the remaining distance. Three-quarters of a half is three-eighths.

So the total sleeping time is one-quarter plus three-eighths which is five-eighths. The portion of time asleep is shown by the coloured areas in the graph.

Start   Finish

I usually sleep for five-eighths of the trip.

15 To make fractions less than 1, the numerator must be less than the denominator. A numerator of 1 can have 6 different denominators (2, 3, 4, 5, 6 or 7). 2 can have 5 different denominators, and so on. As 6 + 5 + 4 + 3 + 2 + 1 = 21, there are 21 possible fractions.

16 The clue to this is to find a number which when multiplied by 3 retains the same digit. When 5 is multiplied by 3 it keeps a 5 in the number. Then a number is needed which, when multiplied by 3 followed by the addition of 1, will also give a 5. Here the number is 8 ($3 \times 8 = 24$; $24 + 1 = 25$). Carry the 2 from this step and now a number is needed which, when multiplied by 3 followed by the addition of 2, gives you 5—obviously this is 1; so X is 1. The sum was $185 \times 3 = 555$.

17 Twenty-five questions answered correctly gives 25 marks and the five errors give minus five marks leaving a score of 20. You know that the number answered correctly plus the number answered incorrectly equals 30 but that the correct number minus the wrong number equals 20 (if $R - W = 20$ and $R + W = 30$, then $2R = 50$ and $R = 25$). If you are not used to solving it like this then don't worry, there is an alternative. You can check the five options to see which one is correct.

18 It doubles its flow every minute, so the minute before 2 hours it is at half its maximum. This is after 1 h 59 min.

19 By drawing horizontal and vertical lines the rectangle can be split into identical triangles. There are 16 triangles, and 8 triangles are unshaded. This means $\frac{1}{2}$ of the rectangle is not shaded.

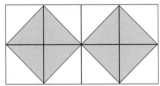

Not to scale

20 As $1 + 4 = 5$, and $115 \div 5 = 23$, the smallest angle is 23°. As $23 \times 4 = 92$, the largest angle is 92°. As $180 - (92 + 23) = 65$, the three angles are 92°, 65° and 23°. The largest is 92°.

21 2 hours 30 minutes is $2\frac{1}{2}$. As $84 \times 2 = 168$ and $\frac{1}{2}$ of 84 is 42, $168 + 42 = 210$. Dante has driven 210 km.

$$\begin{array}{r} 79\,811 \\ +\quad 210 \\ \hline 80\,021 \end{array}$$

The odometer shows 80 021.

22 22×2 gives the cost of the adult tickets. $(22 \times 3) \div 2$ gives the cost of the children's tickets. 5×5 gives the cost of the ice creams. The number sentence is $22 \times 2 + (22 \times 3) \div 2 + 5 \times 5$.

23 As $78 \div 2 = 39$, the sum of the length and width is 39. As the length is always 1 cm longer than the width, the dimensions are 20 cm and 19 cm. As $19 \times 20 = 380$, the area is 380 cm².

24 Three more squares should be shaded.

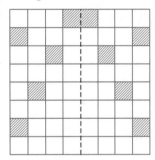

25 As a pineapple has the same mass as 3 oranges, 2 pineapples have the same mass as 6 oranges. As 2 oranges have the same mass as 4 apples, then 6 oranges have the same mass as 12 apples. This means 2 pineapples have the same mass as 12 apples.

26 As $1 - (0.2 + 0.5) = 0.3$, then $\frac{3}{10}$ of the balls are purple. If $0.2 = \frac{2}{10}$ which represents 12 balls, then $\frac{1}{10}$ is 6 balls and $\frac{3}{10} = 18$ balls. There are 18 purple balls.

27 As $32 \div 4 = 8$, the volume of a cube is 8 m³. As $2 \times 2 \times 2 = 8$, each cube has a side length of 2 m. Each square face has an area of $2 \times 2 = 4$, and there are 6 faces. As $6 \times 4 = 24$, the total area is 24 m².

28 As $360 \div 3 \times 4 = 480$, the container holds 480 L when full.

As $\frac{2}{3}$ of 480 is $480 \div 3 \times 2 = 160 \times 2 = 320$, the tank will hold 320 L.

29 As $26 - 20 = 6$, the mass of 5 L of detergent is 6 kg. Multiplying by 4 means the mass of 20 L of detergent is 24 kg. As $26 - 24 = 2$, the mass of the empty container is 2 kg.

30 As $\$22 + \$5 + \$4 + \$2 + 30c + 20c = \$33.50$, Eve has \$33.50 in the jar.

31 $360 \div 8 = 45$, and $3 \times 45 = 135$, so the object has been rotated 135° clockwise.

32 As $8 \times 8 = 64$, the area of the large square is 64 cm². As $2 \times 2 = 4$, the area of each small square is 4 cm². As $64 - 4 \times 4 = 64 - 16 = 48$, the remaining area is 48 cm². This means $\frac{48}{64}$, or $\frac{3}{4}$ of the original square remains.

33 As $(32 - 6 - 6) \div 2 = 10$, the dimensions are 10 cm by 6 cm by 6 cm. As $36 \times 10 = 360$, the volume is 360 cm³.

34 If the missing number is 5, the probability of a factor of 6 is $\frac{4}{8}$ and the probability of a multiple of 2 is $\frac{4}{8}$.

35 As $1 + 7 + 5 + 4 + 2 + 1 = 20$, there were 20 students surveyed. Statement 1 is correct.

As $1 \times 0 + 7 \times 1 + 5 \times 2 + 4 \times 3 + 2 \times 4 + 1 \times 5 = 0 + 7 + 10 + 12 + 8 + 5 = 42$, there was a total of 42 televisions. Statement 2 is correct.

$5 + 4 + 2 + 1 = 12$. This means 12 out of 20 students had at least 2 televisions.

This is $\frac{12}{20} = \frac{60}{100}$, which is 60%. Statement 3 is correct. This means Statements 1, 2 and 3 are correct.

MATHEMATICAL REASONING Test 4 〔Page 83〕

1 A 2 D 3 A 4 B 5 C 6 A 7 C 8 D 9 B
10 D 11 C 12 C 13 B 14 A 15 B 16 C
17 D 18 B 19 A 20 C 21 E 22 A 23 C
24 E 25 B 26 A 27 B 28 D 29 E 30 C
31 E 32 D 33 E 34 E 35 D

1 Together they can make 60 products in an hour. In 25 minutes one worker produces 10 products and the other produces 15 products.

2 There are 40 blocks in the drawing and 64 blocks are required for a cube that is $4 \times 4 \times 4$. As $64 - 40 = 24$, another 24 blocks are needed.

3 The missing number is 8. This involves addition across the row and down each column. The completed square is shown below.

10	8	18
12	18	30
22	26	48

4 Try each of these numbers and you will see that 152 is the correct answer.

5 Line C is one-eighth the length of line A because it is half the length of line B (that is one-quarter of line A).

6 I: $\frac{12 \times \cancel{9} \times \cancel{15}^5}{\cancel{3} \times \cancel{3} \times \cancel{3}}$ and II: $\frac{\cancel{12}^2 \times \cancel{9} \times \cancel{15}^5}{\cancel{6} \times \cancel{9} \times \cancel{3}}$ give whole number answers. This means that I or II would fit with no space left over.

7 The total score of the first group is 400 and the score of the second group is 700. The combined score is 1100 for the 15 pupils, giving an average of about 73.3.

8 The weight of five chocolates is 75 g, so the 15 chocolates weigh 15×15 g or 225 g and the container must then weigh 25 g $(250 - 225)$.

9 Look at the ones column in the addition: as $A + A = A$, then A must equal 0. Now the tens column in the addition: $7 + 8$ is 15, so B must equal 5. Now the hundreds: $1 + C + 6 = 8$ means C equals 1. Also in the thousands column: $1 + D = 5$ means D is 4. Here is the partially solved answer so far:

$$
\begin{array}{r}
U34 \\
\times \quad U5 \\
\hline
1170 \\
4680 \\
\hline
5850 \\
\end{array}
$$

Looking at the multiplication, U must be 2. The completed answer is:

$$
\begin{array}{r}
234 \\
\times \quad 25 \\
\hline
1170 \\
4680 \\
\hline
5850 \\
\end{array}
$$

10 The arrow is just before 53, so the mass is 52.9 kg.

11 There are two face symbols used so this is called a binary number system. Notice that ☺ is 1 more than ☹ and place value is used. Here are the numbers up to 11:

0 = ☹, 1 = ☺, 2 = ☺☹, 3 = ☺☺,
4 = ☺☹☹, 5 = ☺☹☺, 6 = ☺☺☹,
7 = ☺☺☺, 8 = ☺☹☹☹, 9 = ☺☹☹☺,
10 = ☺☹☺☹, 11 = ☺☹☺☺. (If we were just using zeros and ones the numbers up to 11 would be 0, 1, 2 = 10, 3 = 11, 4 = 100, 5 = 101, 6 = 110, 7 = 111, 8 = 1000, 9 = 1001, 10 = 1010, 11 = 1011.)

12 There were 17 stamps altogether and you will need to count from both ends in order to determine this. The bold numbers show the position of the kangaroo stamp which is used as a marker for the counting from both sides:

1 2 3 4 5 6 7 **8**
10 9 8 7 6 5 4 3 2 1

There are 17 stamps in total.

13 You know that the length is three times the width plus 3 cm. So the perimeter is the two widths plus six times the width plus 6 cm. This gives eight times the width plus 6 cm and we know that the total perimeter is 54 cm. So, eight times the width is equal to 54 − 6 = 48 and the width is equal to 6 cm.

14 The seating arrangement for the teachers (T) and parents (P) was:
TPTPTPTPTPTT.

15 The plane arrives at 11 am Adelaide time which is 11.30 am Sydney time.

16 The differences between the numbers are: 4, 14, 24, 34 etc. As 97 − 34 = 63, the missing number is 63.

17 On day one the student revised 81 questions; day two 54 questions; day three 36 questions; day four 24 questions; day five 16 questions.

18 $\frac{50}{2} \times 50 + \frac{50}{2} = 25 \times 50 + 25 = 1250 + 25$
$= 1275$

19 Their ages are 11 and 16 years. Take each option in turn and think about what combinations of numbers add up to say 27 that would also multiply to give 176. Some of the larger and smaller numbers can be easily excluded. If a

question like this takes too much time maybe you might want to take a guess then come back to it later.

20 Only the cubes in the two middle and interior rows have face-to-face contact with six other cubes. There are eight interior cubes.

21 In the first round there are eight matches and the eight winners will go on to play four matches; the four winners will play two matches; and the finalist will play the last match. This makes 8 + 4 + 2 + 1 = 15. As there is one winner there are 15 losers. This means there had to be 15 matches to produce 15 losers.

22 The numbers of products are 2 A; 15 B; 5 C; 6 D; and 2 Rejects.

23 There are three shapes.: circle, octagon and hexagon.

24 The entire graph (360°) represents 72 students. As 360 − (120 + 150) = 90, and $\frac{90}{360} = \frac{1}{4}$, then one-quarter of the students have red or black hair. As 72 ÷ 4 = 18, there are 18 students.

25 3 over when divided by 5 means the number ends in a 3 or 8. 4 over when divided by 6 means the number is even. Looking for a number between 30 and 80 ending in 8 gives 58, as 58 ÷ 5 = 11, remainder 3 and 58 ÷ 6 = 9, remainder 4.

26 As 40 ÷ 4 = 10, the length of each side of the smaller squares is 10 cm. When formed, the large square has side length 30 cm. As 30 × 30 = 900, the area is 900 cm².

27 The square G4 is not on the image.

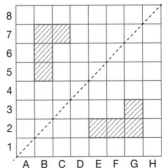

28 On Saturday there were 76 cups and Wednesday 38 cups. As $38 \times 2 = 76$, twice as many cups were used on Saturday compared to Wednesday. Statement 1 is correct.

As $36 + 28 + 38 = 102$, there were 102 cups used. Statement 2 is correct. $28 + 38 = 66$ and $48 + 70 = 118$. As $118 - 56 = 52$, there were 52 fewer cups used. Statement 3 is not correct. Statements 1 and 2 are correct statements.

29 Look for a number that is 1 more than a multiple of 5, 6 and 8. As $5 \times 6 \times 8 = 240$ is a multiple, so too is 120. The number is 121.

30 Using order of operation rules,
$[120 - 48 \div 4 \times 8 - 4] \div 20 =$
$[120 - 96 - 4] \div 20 = 20 \div 20 = 1$.

31 The rule is adding 7. The numbers are 2, 9, 16, 23, 30, 37 … The first number is 2.
As $2 + 49 \times 7 = 2 + 343 = 345$, the 50th number is 345.

32 There are 12 letters around the spinner. From T to X in a clockwise direction is 8 letters. This is two-thirds of a revolution. As $360 \div 3 \times 2 = 240$, the angle is 240°.

33 If the first number removed was 1, 3 or 5, the probability of the second number being less than 6 is the same as the probability that it is odd. If the first number removed was 6 or 8, the probability of the second number being less than 6 is the same as the probability that it is odd. From the options, the number was 8.

34 As $16 \times 16 \div 2 = 16 \times 8 = 128$, the area of each of the rectangles is 128 cm². The small triangle has a base of 8 cm and a height of 8 cm. As $128 - \frac{1}{2} \times 8 \times 8 = 128 - 32 = 96$, the shaded area is 96 cm².

35 The possible scores are $1 \times 3 = 3$, $1 \times 3 = 3$, $1 \times 2 = 2$, $4 \times 3 = 12$, $4 \times 3 = 12$, $4 \times 2 = 8$, $5 \times 3 = 15$, $5 \times 3 = 15$, $5 \times 2 = 10$, $6 \times 3 = 18$, $6 \times 3 = 18$ and $6 \times 2 = 12$. The scores are 3, 3, 2, 12, 12, 8, 15, 15, 10, 18, 18 and 12. The highest score is 18. Statement 1 is correct. There are 12 scores and there are three 12s. This means the probability of a score of 12 is $\frac{1}{4}$.

Statement 2 is correct. There are 8 scores greater than 8, and 8 even scores. As they are equally likely, Statement 3 is correct. Statements 1, 2 and 3 are correct.

Answers

Writing tests

Structure

Audience

The topic is one that would be familiar to readers. The writer quickly specifies the location and a time frame.

An issue to be resolved is introduced.

The text is written in the first person (I).

Text structure

Time of the year is used to show reasons for the situation.

The story has an easy-to-follow chronological sequence.

The narrative focuses on specific events.

Paragraphing

New paragraphs are used for changes in speakers, time and place.

Cohesion

The writer's intention is established early.

The situation now seems hopeless.

Tension between the characters is maintained throughout the text.

The story has an obvious beginning, middle and end.

The final sentences demonstrate quickly how the problem was solved in a satisfying way for the reader.

The narrative moves from excitement to increasing desperation to a somewhat predictable conclusion.

The coda (final sentences) neatly rounds off the narrative with a reference to sighing.

Language and ideas

Vocabulary

Good use is made of unusual words, adverbs, verbs and adjectives.

Sentence structure

A wide variety of sentence beginnings and lengths is included.

Direct speech keeps the storyline flowing.

Most sentences are statements.

Ideas

The interplay of characters' speech in the dialogue is clear.

Repetition of 'sighed' highlights Krystal's frustration.

Punctuation

Clear use is made of speech marks.

Questions highlight the sense of exasperation felt.

Exclamation marks increase the sense of urgency to make a decision.

Short sentences are used for dramatic effect.

A reference to a sound adds authenticity to the narrative and contributes to the character's feelings.

Spelling

There are no spelling errors of common, unusual or technical words.

Jasper and the Snowman

I sighed. Then I sighed again as I looked out across our lawn. The July school hols had hardly started and I was already totally bored.

'Krystal, stop sighing and find something to do!' growled my father.

'Can't do anything. It's snowing,' I sighed. The front lawn was deep in snow. It was one of the biggest falls the Blue Mountains had seen in years. I should be impressed.

I could just make out Jasper's clomping through the gloom of drifting snowflakes. Bet Jasper's found something to do, I thought grudgingly.

As he arrived at the front door, I had an idea.

'Want to build a snowman?' I suddenly exclaimed as if it was a brilliant idea.

Jasper put his head to one side. He definitely wasn't expecting that question. 'Right. Okay,' he agreed cautiously.

'Why not?' I fired at him.

'Mine always fall over!'

I couldn't believe it! Jasper who knew everything about snow couldn't make an upright snowman.

'We'll make it lying down. Can't fall over then!' I said slickly. For a smart kid Jasper never thinks of the obvious. Too much book learning to be practical.

I'll show Dad, I thought. I wasn't sure what. A horizontal snowman was not a great creation. Correct! Our snowman was a disaster. Jasper is not renowned for his artistic streak and he wasn't keen on any of my ideas.

'We could give him something to read,' I said brightly. 'Like he's reading in bed?'

Jasper screwed up the corner of his mouth.

'We could give him sunglasses,' I suggested meekly. 'Like he's lying on the beach sunbaking?'

Jasper hunched his shoulders and looked at the air-drenched snow. That said enough!

In the distance a freight train blew its sad, lonesome whistle as it crawled west over the mountains to Lithgow. It seemed to match my mood.

Our snowman really looked like several barrow loads of snow had been dumped on the lawn in a rough line. He had a stick nose and a hole for a mouth and one for each ear.

Pathetic, I thought.

Jasper said rather timidly, picking up on my hostile vibes, 'Probably the wrong sort of snow …'

I harrumphed my disbelief. Jasper turned and headed off through the snow. I sighed and headed indoors.

Language and ideas

Vocabulary
Alliteration is used in the headline.
Effective use of unusual words: adverbs, verbs and adjectives.
Scientific terms provide authenticity.
A personal reaction is included.

Sentence structure
Italics are used for emphasis.
A wide variety of sentence beginnings is used.
Advice for those finding injured birds is logical and clear.
Capital letters are used correctly for proper nouns and acronyms.
Indirect speech is used correctly.
Most sentences are statements, both simple and compound.

Ideas
The text balances personal reaction with professional facts.

Punctuation
Effective use is made of commas.
Some restrained use of exclamations is included.
The last line rounds off the point made in the first line and gives a context to the efforts of volunteers

Spelling
There are no spelling errors of common or unusual words.

Raptor Rescue

Tucked behind a small ridge west of the Great Dividing Range is a large native animal rescue site. One of the special buildings is a large aviary housing four injured wedge-tailed eagles.

These raptors spend their days recuperating: resting, eating and learning to fly again until they are strong enough to be released back into the wild.

Dr Justine Bush, manager of the facility, said that for her and the wildlife carers releasing the raptors is one of the best feelings the staff experiences. The birds seem to glance back before embracing their new freedom.

Most sick or injured raptors found by people are collision victims. A sick or head-injured raptor will sit drooping its head and looking fluffed up. In contrast, an otherwise injured raptor is sleek until you get close when it may puff its feathers as a threat.

Limiting stress to the raptor is *the* priority, Dr Bush advises. Wild birds are often killed by shock rather than their injuries.

Raptors are at the apex of the food chain. Healthy apex predators mean a healthier ecosystem.

If a mature raptor allows you to approach it, it may be in shock or badly injured. Don't subject the bird to extra stress by trying to get hold of it.

Raptors are powerful animals. Even the smallest species, such as kestrels, have astounding power in their feet and talons. Raptors flip onto their backs and present their talons, their most dangerous weapons, to hurt their enemies. It is important that you pick up the raptor gingerly.

Do not place raptors in wire cages! Wire damages the feathers and cere (a waxy covering at the base of the upper beak) and makes the raptor unreleasable. Place the raptor in a darkened cardboard carton perforated with holes along its sides near the bottom, lined with newspaper or a towel. Never add straw or sawdust and do not place water or food in the carton. Try to keep the bird cool.

Take the injured raptor to your local wildlife carer/rehabilitation group, such as WIRES in NSW or the RSPCA. Those involved in raptor rehabilitation use raptor hoods. These hoods help sedate the bird and prevent it from injuring itself.

The wedge-tailed eagle is Australia's largest raptor. Will it still be around for future generations?

Adapted from https://ausraptorgroup.org/captive-raptors

Structure

Audience
The audience is readers interested in the environment and wildlife rescue.
The writer quickly establishes the issue and the actual location.
The goals of the organisation are outlined.

Text structure
The article deals with a scientific issue.
Points are raised to give credence to the relevance of the article.
The article is written in the past tense.
Professional opinion is included.
The report focuses on specific information.

Paragraphing
Paragraphs are short and focus on one point but may include some support detail.
Topic sentences are used to introduce some paragraphs.

Cohesion
The writer's intention is established early: to inform in an objective manner.
The final paragraphs stress the importance of the rescue work being done.
The text ends with a rhetorical question to engage with the reader.

Language and ideas

Vocabulary

Good use is made of verbs and adjectives.

A strong positive tone is used to state the writer's case.

Colloquial terms help the reader identify with the arguments made.

Sentence structure

A wide variety of sentence beginnings is used.

Most sentences are statements, with a mixture of simple and compound sentences.

Ideas

Exclamations are used for dramatic effect.

A simile gives a clear picture of the writer's dismay.

Ideas are well articulated to create a sense of rational, logical argument.

Rhetorical questions keep the reader engaged.

Questions are used to highlight the writer's frustrations.

Punctuation

There is controlled use of exclamations and italics.

Exclamation marks increase the sense of urgency to make a decision.

Other punctuation, including apostrophes, commas and full stops, is correctly applied.

Spelling

There are no spelling errors of common or unusual words.

Should beach driving be disallowed?

Australia's magnificent beaches of unspoilt beauty and attractive climate are great places to fish, swim, camp, explore, view the scenery or simply 'get away from it all'.

For many adults, beach driving gives a sense of freedom and gets them to places less visited. Remote beaches provide access to great fishing and camping spots. Kite-surfers or fishing enthusiasts can transport heavy gear without trekking distances across soft sand.

For off-road enthusiasts, a relaxing beach drive in warm weather may seem an innocent enough activity. Why try to disallow it?

For the nesting shorebirds who make their homes along the coastline it's another story.

For many shore birds, such as terns, stilts and plovers, the warm weather is when they nest. Beach vehicles can crush delicate eggs and run over small chicks. New chicks are well camouflaged and are not seen by drivers! The chicks can easily fall into the deep unstable ruts made by off-road tyre tracks along the shoreline and get stuck. Worse still, vehicles may roll over a chick while it is trapped like a rabbit in a hole.

Beach driving can be frightening and disruptive to nesting adult birds, who may fly off when a vehicle roars down the beach.

Chicks and eggs become exposed to temperature stress and to predators: crows, seagulls, foxes, feral pigs and cats. If parenting birds are disturbed too often, a colony may choose to abandon the site. Do the beach drivers take this into account? I don't think so!

Endangered marine turtles use our beaches as nesting sites between November and April each year. These are the warmer months enjoyed by the beach-vehicle tourist.

On isolated shorelines there is no-one to deter drivers from venturing onto nearby dunes. Dune bashing is seen by some as an adventure sport. Can you believe some may even think of dunes as scrub?

Rare reptiles, insects and birds live in the dunes and between the tide lines. Driving in these areas creates problems for them. Crabs and shellfish that live under the sand have little chance of escaping.

Beach driving can contribute to habitat degradation. It can contribute to beach erosion and certainly harms the fragile dune vegetation, which is important for stabilising our beautiful beaches.

Beach driving? Call it beach bashing!

Structure

Audience

The topic is one that could be an issue for families with environmental concerns, as well as those who like access to off-road activities.

The writer quickly and forcefully establishes the issue and implies their stance.

Personal comments are written in the first person (I).

Text structure

Points are organised sequentially and logically.

The text contains a well organised introduction, support points and a conclusion.

Emotive words are used throughout the text (endangered, bashing, roars, rolls).

Paragraphing

New paragraphs are used for each new point.

Topic sentences are used to introduce the paragraph's main idea.

Cohesion

The writer's intention is established early.

The writer refers regularly to words used in the topic.

The text is mostly written in the past tense.

Personal experience is used to bolster the position taken.

The final paragraph refers to the topic and re-establishes how the writer feels.

The text ends with a strong, personal reaffirmation of the writer's opinion.

The concluding sentences round off the stance taken in the opening paragraph.

Language and ideas

Vocabulary
Good use is made of unusual words, adverbs, verbs and adjectives.

Casual language helps the reader identify with the narrator.

Sentence structure
A wide variety of sentence beginnings is included.

Statements are a mixture of simple and complex sentences.

Ideas
Exclamations are used for dramatic effect.

A simile gives a clear picture of the writer's amusement.

Coarse language is used by the labourer.

Recount ideas are well articulated and sequenced to create a sense of relevant observations.

Specific location and time facts provide the reader with a clear mental picture.

Punctuation
There is controlled use of direct speech, exclamations and italics.

A common saying gives an insight into the character.

Other punctuation, including commas, apostrophes and full stops, is correctly applied.

Spelling
There are no spelling errors of common, unusual or technical words.

The Antique Store

(Tiana, her mother and the narrator visit an antique store. Now read on.)

Pitt's Antiques and Collectibles store looked like it should be in a collection. It was certainly a building jam-packed with — junk! A window sign announced: LATEST ANTIQUES AVAILABLE.

On that Friday, when Mrs Brown entered the store she immediately headed for a dark, musty corner full of trays of tarnished silverware. She collects teaspoons. Meanwhile we wandered around the grotty aisles. Suddenly I spotted a teapot that looked like a toilet seat. How would people feel about drinking tea made in a pot like that? Still, it was unusual.

In a back corner a burly man in a black singlet was loading wooden crates onto a trolley. I peered at the crates. They would be the right size for a stack of coffins. Surely not! That idea was just too silly!

Before I could say anything, Black-Singlet scowled at us and said gruffly, 'No customers in this area. It's da rule!'

'I just wanted to speak to Mr Pitt and—' I started.

'Youse'll find him up front!' he snarled.

We retreated quickly to Mr Pitt's front desk.

'We're looking for information. About collecting things,' I said politely as we approached the desk.

The only response was a frown.

'We saw you on telly. *The Antique Show*,' Tiana stated. 'What do people collect?'

Then Mr Pitt stood up tall. He pursed his lips before replying. 'No answer to that — or a million answers. People collect anything. People collect cars or soft-drink cans or bottles. Teddy bears, teacups, old toys. You name it — you can collect it!'

'Does it have to be old?' I asked.

He paused for a moment before answering. 'Odd or old. If it's old, you find bargains in street markets or garage sales. Trash or treasure's the name of the game. Someone's trash is another person's treasure. It's a bit late to take an interest in numismatics or become a philatelist.' Another big smile.

'Coins and stamps,' muttered Tiana.

Structure

Audience
The topic is one that would be familiar to students and parents.

The writer firmly establishes the who, what and where of the topic.

The text is written in the first person (*We*, *I*).

Text structure
Points are organised chronologically.

The text contains a brief introduction, followed by progress points and a conclusion.

An oxymoron is used to reinforce the amusing tone of the passage.

Paragraphing
New paragraphs are used for changes in time.

Topic sentences are used to introduce the main idea of a paragraph

Cohesion
The writer refers regularly to words used in the topic.

The text is witty and written in the past tense.

Personal reactions bolster the stance taken.

The final paragraph refers to the topic and re-establishes how the narrator's feelings evolved.

The text concludes with an explanation of technical terms.

Tiana's last comment gently mocks Mr Pitt.

WRITING CHECKLISTS

Checklist for writing narratives

 Page 88

Did the student:

- write at least one sentence to orient readers and capture their imagination?
- include a 'catchy' beginning?
- include an event that adds interest to the story and makes it worth telling?
- resolve the story in a satisfying way?
- use vivid, interesting images to describe people, places, things and activities, such as verbs, adverbs and adjectives?
- use appropriate grammar, punctuation and spelling?
- include a variety of sentence beginnings and lengths?
- use figurative literary techniques such as similes, metaphors, alliteration, rhetorical questions and repetition?
- include relevant descriptions?
- make the narrative flow?
- create ongoing tension to make the reader want to read on?
- provide a satisfying conclusion?
- have a handwriting style that was legible?

Checklist for writing newspaper reports

 Page 89

Did the student:

- choose an interesting subject/topic?
- generate a 'catchy' headline?
- orient readers to who, what, where and when?
- write in the past tense?
- use the third person?
- use short, well-spaced paragraphs?
- include interesting details?
- use vivid, interesting images to describe people, places, things and activities, such as verbs, adverbs and adjectives?
- use appropriate grammar, punctuation and spelling?
- add personal comments and/or comments by interested parties about what happened?
- distinguish between direct speech and reported speech?
- use time words and expressions to allow the reader to follow the sequence of events?
- use figurative journalistic techniques such as similes, metaphors, alliteration, rhetorical questions and repetition?
- write a concluding comment?
- have a handwriting style that was legible?

WRITING CHECKLISTS

Checklist for writing persuasive texts

Page 90

Did the student:

- make the issue clear from the beginning?
- provide a clear statement of their opinion (using the first person)?
- make their points flow clearly and logically?
- develop arguments using facts and examples?
- arouse any feelings or reactions in the reader?
- use clear paragraphs for each point?
- use appropriate grammar, punctuation and spelling?
- use personal pronouns correctly?
- include a variety of sentence beginnings?
- use interesting verbs, adverbs and adjectives?
- use figurative literary techniques such as similes, metaphors, alliteration, rhetorical questions and repetition?
- make you want to read on?
- suggest and challenge any alternative opinions?
- restate the original assertion clearly as part of the conclusion?
- have a handwriting style that was legible?

Checklist for writing recounts

Page 91

Did the student:

- quickly let readers know where, when and who was involved?
- include an intriguing/interesting location?
- include incidents that add interest to the recount and make it worth retelling?
- provide a thought-provoking conclusion?
- use vivid, interesting images to describe people, places, things and activities, such as verbs, adverbs and adjectives?
- use appropriate grammar, punctuation and spelling?
- include a variety of sentence beginnings and lengths?
- use some figurative literary techniques such as similes, metaphors, alliteration, rhetorical questions and repetition?
- incorporate some factual text to provide a sense of authenticity?
- include relevant descriptions?
- include chronological features (e.g. adverbs of time) that keep the narrative flowing?
- create an ongoing issue to encourage readers to read on?
- make the characters realistic?
- have a handwriting style that was legible?

NOTES

NOTES